The Woman's Fix-It Book

INCREDIBLY SIMPLE

WEEKEND PROJECTS AND EVERYDAY HOME REPAIR

The Woman's Fix-It Book

INCREDIBLY SIMPLE
WEEKEND PROJECTS AND EVERYDAY HOME REPAIR

Karen Dale Dustman

Illustrated by Cindi Dixon and Eva Stina Bender

CHANDLER HOUSE PRESS

Worcester, Massachusetts

1998

The Woman's Fix-It Book:
Incredibly Simple Weekend Projects and Everyday Home Repair

Copyright ©1998 by Karen Dale Dustman

ISBN 1-886284-14-8
Library of Congress Catalog Card Number 97-77694
First Edition
ABCDEFGHIJK

PUBLISHED BY
Chandler House Press
335 Chandler Street
Worcester, MA 01602
USA

PRESIDENT
Lawrence J. Abramoff

PUBLISHER/EDITOR-IN-CHIEF
Richard J. Staron

VICE PRESIDENT OF SALES
Irene S. Bergman

EDITORIAL/PRODUCTION MANAGER
Jennifer J. Goguen

BOOK & COVER DESIGN
Marshall Henrichs

ILLUSTRATIONS
Cindi Dixon and Eva Stina Bender

Chandler House Press books are available at special discounts for bulk purchases. For more information about how to arrange such purchases, please contact Irene Bergman at Chandler House Press, 335 Chandler Street, Worcester, MA 01602, or call (800) 642-6657, or fax (508) 756-9425, or find us on the World Wide Web at www.tatnuck.com.

Chandler House Press books are distributed to the trade by
National Book Network, Inc.
4720 Boston Way
Lanham, MD 20706
(800) 462-6420

DISCLAIMER:

This book is intended to provide a general introduction to common household maintenance projects, but we cannot of course offer definitive advice about any and all situations that you may encounter. There is no substitute for competent, in-person professional assistance.

We also don't presume to advise you about local building codes, which can and do vary considerably across the nation. Always consult your local building department for guidance before starting any repair or home improvement project. In some cases, a permit and inspection of the work may be necessary.

One final word about risks and responsibility: there's danger anywhere in life these days — even a task as simple as crossing the street has pitfalls. Certainly some of the repair projects discussed in this book (those involving electricity or climbing ladders, for example) involve some element of potential risk. You're an adult and, we must assume, a reasonably intelligent and prudent one. We've tried to flag areas where a precautionary step like shutting off circuit breakers may help. However, the publisher and author cannot and do not assume responsibility for any damage, harm or injury caused by or related to repair efforts or techniques described in this book.

We strongly advise you to call in a licensed professional if you have any questions about your own skills and abilities to successfully undertake a project. Take care, and work safely.

Acknowledgments

No man is an island and no book (at least, none worth reading) is created in a vacuum. I owe a tremendous debt of gratitude to Dick and Rick Dustman, Greg and Janet Langsfeld, Brenda and Bruce Gordon, and Dick Neyman for their patient fielding of innumerable questions, careful manuscript reading, and many helpful suggestions. Heartfelt appreciation is also due to computer genius Ed Wozniak for a battery of wonderful web-site finds. Thank you to Dale Hart, president of the San Antonio Pioneer Council, for proofing the telephone section, and to Cathy Strasnick and Dave Thompson of the National Lead Information Center, who were exceedingly generous with information and suggestions for the lead hazards section. And a hearty *gracias* to my ever-patient and gracious agent, Bert Holtje, for believing in this project.

To Carol Turkington, who cheered me on from first flash of inspiration to final flourish, words of thanks seem hardly enough. This book owes its life to you.

CONTENTS

INTRODUCTION

When I was a kid, our entire tool collection consisted of a couple of screwdrivers, one lonely hammer and some twine — all buried in the chaos of a kitchen drawer. I remember our family gathering in awe as Dad hooked up rabbit ears to our TV set. But that's about as technical as things ever got.

Not that we were without practical skills. Mom taught us how to follow a recipe and decipher a dress pattern. And getting the tension right on that balky old Singer sewing machine required an engineer's precision and a mechanic's touch.

But when a toilet broke or a bedroom needed paint, there was only one solution. We called someone.

Today the garage I share with my ever-patient husband is bulging at the seams with construction detritus — electrical wire, plumbing parts, scraps of molding, and enough leftover paint to float a small battleship. Many of the tools (and somehow, I tease him, the *only* tools either of us can find) are mine.

I learned how to fix things the hard way: by owning rentals. There were holes in the walls and holes in the floor, plumbing leaks and plumbing someone else had "fixed." Windows, jambs and doors got broken. And everything, it seemed, was constantly in need of paint.

I watched over a boyfriend's shoulder (an ex-boyfriend, my husband is happy to note), and figured out that most of this stuff really wasn't all that hard. We graduated from renovating rentals to building a couple of new houses. I swept floors, ran for parts, and helped stand newly-framed walls. I learned to do the wiring because it was cheaper than hiring an electrician. A few years later I bought a "quaint" little house of my own, which taught me a few things of its own about plumbing.

The moral of the story (besides run for cover should anyone try to interest you in a "quaint" house) is this: household repairs aren't rocket science. You needn't have learned any of it at your father's — or mother's — knee; you can acquire what you need to know, project by project. And you'll gain confidence as you go along.

Perhaps you have an itch to hang your own miniblinds, or you are newly single and facing a recalcitrant toilet. Maybe you're moving into your first apartment, or you find your once-helpful husband now irresistibly glued to the couch on weekends.

Whether you're tired of waiting for someone else to un-stick the garbage disposal or simply eager to erase all evidence of a previous occupant's fascination with chartreuse paint, this book is for you.

So dig in and enjoy. There's nothing quite as satisfying as a job well-done — especially one you've done yourself!

How to Use This Book

This book is designed for first-timers — you don't need any special skills, background, or training. We take you through each project, step by step.

To help you successfully tackle each fix-it project, a list of the necessary tools and parts is provided directly below each chapter head. We suggest you read through the entire section before you start, to get a "feel" for the project. And you'll want to pay special attention to any **"cautions and caveats"** notes, alerting you to potential pitfalls.

You'll also find little **"call in an expert"** phones sprinkled throughout the text. These help you identify situations in which it may be best to check with a knowledgeable friend or professional before proceeding.

One general caution: local building codes and requirements can vary. We've tried to give you general guidance that should be appropriate in most situations. But it pays to know the rules in your particular city or county. Always check with your local building department to determine whether a permit is required before beginning any plumbing, electrical, or structural work.

The projects in this book can be undertaken in any order. Check the index, if necessary, for help in finding the proper page. While you probably already know what a hammer and putty knife look like, we've included line drawings of other tools in the Glossary to help you identify any strangers.

There's no right place to start in the book, but there is a right time — now!! So turn to a project that you'd like to tackle, and let's get started!

Recommendations for a Basic Home Repair Kit

Plumbing:

- 2 crescent wrenches (one medium, one small)
- adjustable (channel joint) pliers
- 2 pipe wrenches (one large, one small)
- allen wrench set
- hacksaw
- basin wrench★
- hand-held snake/drain cleaner
- plumber's putty
- teflon tape
- propane torch★

Electrical:

- 2 Phillips screwdrivers (one large, one small)
- 2 flat-blade screwdrivers (one large, one small)
- miniature screwdriver
- electrical tester to check for live wires
- wire strippers
- dikes (diagonal pliers)
- needlenose pliers
- blunt-nosed pliers
- wire nuts (assorted)
- electrical tape
- "hope chest" box

Painting:

- roller
- roller handle extension
- brush
- paint tray
- screen for 5-gallon paint bucket
- putty knife
- sanding block
- spackle

Miscellaneous:

- screw gun★ (in my opinion, you're better off to pass on the smaller, electric screwdriver variety; it's worth the extra money for one with some real power)
- hammer (claw-type)
- drill
- drill index★ containing selection of high-speed drill bits
- measuring tape
- studfinder
- utility knife with retractable blade
- level
- flashlight
- extension cord with 3-prong (grounded) plug

★ Tools marked with an (★) are "ups and extras" — helpful but not essential for a basic tool kit.

You will undoubtedly collect more tools as you go along, but this list will give you a place to start.

As you will quickly discover, there is a wide range of prices for what look like virtually the same tool. But as with most things, you get what you pay for. Cheap tools can let you down when you least need another headache. My advice is to buy the very best tools you can afford. Consider them investments that will pay for themselves time and time again.

Keeping your tools in separate totes by category (plumbing, electrical, etc.) can help you stay organized — and find the right tool more easily. You may also want to purchase divided organizer boxes for screws, plumbing parts, and other small items.

One of the best tips anyone ever gave me was to start a "hope chest" — a can of spare parts that you "hope" will contain the perfect widget to bail you out in an emergency. My own hope chest is a miniature coffee can with a battered plastic lid that rides around permanently in my box of electrical tools. Inside is a wildly eclectic and constantly changing mish-mash of nails, screws, wire nuts, threaded caps for light fixtures, flat washers and other leftover bits and pieces.

I can't tell you how many times I've emptied that little can, hoping against hope to find something that will save me another run to the hardware store — and discovered the exact part I needed (or one close enough to work)!

Start a spare parts hope chest with your very first project — any small, unbreakable container with a reasonably secure lid will do. Throw in those extra drywall screws and the leftover wire nut you don't know what to do with. Next week, when you run across an elderly metal washer and a couple of finish nails, add them to the pot. You'll be glad you did.

The Woman's Fix-It Book

INCREDIBLY SIMPLE

WEEKEND PROJECTS AND EVERYDAY HOME REPAIR

Chapter 1

ELECTRICAL PROJECTS

Basic Concepts

You probably already know more than you think about the electrical system in your house. The basics are really pretty simple. Power comes in from your utility company through wires that attach to the house either at a pole on the roof, or through an underground feed. Either way, the power is transferred to your main electrical panel (or "box"), which contains the utility company's favorite device: the meter.

The Panel & Breakers

The electrical panel does the job of distributing power to the various "circuits." A circuit will provide power to a series of outlets or light fixtures, or to one important appliance such as the refrigerator or dishwasher.

The panel also performs an extremely important safety function: it contains fuses or breakers to "break" the electrical flow to each circuit in case of a short (caused, for example, by an unwary human touching a live wire).

Perhaps most important of all, the electrical panel contains a MAIN SHUT-OFF to disable power to all circuits at once.

Take a moment right now to peek inside your electrical panel. If you don't already know where it is, look to see where the power lines attach to your roof. The electrical panel is usually located directly below that power "drop." If your power comes in via an underground feed, look for a pipe coming up from the ground to a metal box attached to the side of the house.

When you open the panel, you will see a series of switches (breakers) OR a series of round (screw-in) or cylindrical fuses. As we've mentioned, these "break" or control the power to the various house circuits.

⚠ CAUTIONS & CAVEATS:

• For safety's sake, wear rubber-soled shoes and always make sure you are standing on a DRY surface when opening the electrical panel. If the ground in front of the panel is damp, or if you'll be standing on concrete (which conducts electricity well), find a piece of lumber to stand on to help insulate you from the ground.

• Be careful not to touch water pipes, appliances, or anything metal that might "ground" you as you work near the panel (or near any other source of electricity, for that matter).

Wires and connecting bars are typically hidden behind a metal partition inside the panel, so only the circuit breakers or fuses should be exposed when you open the panel lid. If that is NOT the case, stop here and **call in an expert!** It's dangerous to be poking around near potentially live wires.

Hopefully, someone will have already labeled the panel so you'll know which switch or fuse controls which portion of the house's electrical system. Look for a list inside the front cover or tags beside each breaker that say things like "kitchen outlets" or "bedroom lights," for example. If there are no labels, procure a helper and follow the instructions in the sidebar on page 5 to identify each circuit for future reference.

The panel will also contain a main breaker. Often (but not always) it is located at the top of the panel. It may look like two breakers with the switch bars tied together. Sometimes it is painted red. Fuse boxes sometimes have a pull-out main or a lever on the outside of the panel. If you are unable to determine which is your "main" breaker, stop for now until you can get someone to assist in identifying it. Some (very old) panels may not *have* a main breaker. If that's the case, it's time to think about hiring an electrician to install a new panel!

When breakers are "tripped" by an overload in the circuit, the breaker switch moves away from the "on" position. It may or may not make it all the way to "off." If you find that more than one light or

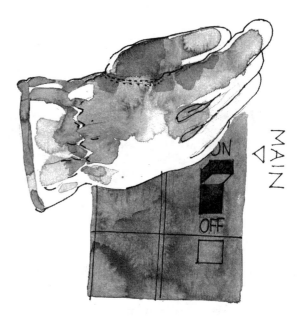

Shutting off main breakers at the panel

Breaker positions

outlet is not working in your house, it's a good bet that you've simply tripped a circuit breaker. Look for a breaker that is in a different position than (out of alignment with) others in the box. Flip the switch firmly all the way to "off," then back to "on." (If you have one breaker that trips repeatedly, see the sidebar that follows on Diagnosing Breaker Troubles.)

If a circuit breaker feels wobbly when you try to flip the switch back on, STOP and **call an expert.** The breaker may have popped loose from its mounting bracket, or the breaker may be damaged and need to be replaced.

Unlike breakers, fuses that have suffered an overload will need to be replaced. (For the screw-in-type fuse, you'll be able to see that the filament has melted by looking through the little window in the fuse.) Replacing a fuse is usually a sim-

Diagnosing Breaker Troubles

If you have one circuit breaker that trips repeatedly, it could indicate one of three possible problems.

First, you may simply have overloaded the circuit by using too many things that draw power at once. Unplug everything on that circuit (or if it is a lighting circuit, turn all lights off), re-set the breaker, and see if that has fixed the problem. Add appliances back one at a time to determine the limit. In my old kitchen, for example, you couldn't use the toaster oven and microwave at the same time. We considered re-wiring the kitchen or getting used to it. (We got used to it.)

Another possible cause of breaker trouble is a short in a particular appliance or an excessive draw for the amperage of the breaker. If the breaker trips every time that appliance is used, that's a pretty good indicator that the appliance is the problem. Try plugging it in on a different circuit; if the breaker now trips on *that* circuit, you may need to have the appliance repaired. (If you have a fuse box, DON'T simply replace the problem fuse with a higher-amperage one!)

Finally, there could be bare wires touching or some other form of short somewhere in the household wiring on that circuit. If you've ruled out the first two possibilities, it's definitely time to **call in an expert!**

ple matter of screwing in a new replacement or popping in a new cartridge-type fuse. (*Be extra careful with cartridge-type fuses!* Their exposed metal ends can conduct electricity from the mounting bracket. You will want to shut down the main breaker before changing a fuse, just as a precaution.)

Be sure to use a replacement fuse with the same amperage as the one you are replacing. For safety's sake, never try to "fix" the problem by using a higher-amperage replacement fuse, or by inserting a penny or another substitute in the fuse-holder; if fuses are blowing, there's a reason.

The Story on Wire

Wire, of course, conducts electricity. But to keep that electricity from zapping everything the wire comes in contact with, the wiring in your house is insulated. In older houses, you may find "cloth" insulation, which looks like fabric wrapped around the wire. Newer wiring will be plastic-coated.

You will probably never need to know exactly what size wire is required for a particular electrical application. But in general, the larger the diameter of wire, the more reliably it conducts electricity from one point to another, without a drop in "oomph." If you've ever tried to run a power tool on a very, VERY long extension cord, you'll know that there is a certain amount of voltage drop as you get farther away from the source. A bigger-diameter wire will help offset this effect.

Just for your future reference, the two most common wire sizes you are likely to encounter are Number 14, which is typically used to wire light fixtures and switches; and Number 12, a slightly heavier-gauge wire used to provide power to outlets.

Hot, Neutral & Ground

Think of electricity like water: it has to *flow* to get from Point A to Point B. That is a tremendous oversimplification, and you engineers in the class can chuckle as you exchange witty remarks about coulombs and potentiation. For the rest of us, electricity is simple if you'll just remember "flow."

Typical household wiring includes three wires in a plastic sheath

Flow requires an inlet AND an outlet. If you stop up the drain in your tub and turn on the tap, you'll soon have a bathtub full of water. But until you open the drain, there is no flow.

The wiring in your house operates on the same principle. Not only do you need power coming IN, you also need a "drain" channel so that the electricity can flow OUT along the wire (lighting appliances and running air conditioners on its way).

In the hundred or so years that we've had electricity in our houses, electricians have evolved some standard terminology and color conventions. The wire that brings power into a circuit or appliance is known as the "hot" wire, and is generally black. The "drain" or "power out" wire is generally white, and (for reasons that remain an utter mystery to me) is referred to as the "neutral" wire.

There's also a third wire you'll find in most houses built after about 1945, known as a "ground." Think of it as a stand-by exit to channel the raging flow in an emergency. As its name implies, the ground wire ultimately leads to a rod buried in the ground somewhere in or near your foundation. The ground wire carries power only in an emergency, and is typically bare (uninsulated) copper. Screws meant for attaching a ground wire are usually (and, for once, logically) green.

CAUTIONS & CAVEATS:

- Electricity can be dangerous. ALWAYS turn power off at the main shut-off on the circuit breaker or fuse panel before beginning an electrical project of any kind. As an extra precaution, consider taping a note to the panel explaining that the power is off on purpose, so that a well-meaning household member doesn't come along and flip the main back on.

- Do NOT touch wires, connectors or shiny bars inside your main electrical panel, even if the main breaker is in the OFF position. *Household circuits may be disabled, but there will still be power to the box itself.* (To disconnect all power to the box, you would need to call your electric company and/or a licensed electrician.)

- Don't hesitate to ask for help if you need it. There are a zillion variations on the wiring theme. Older houses, in particular, can contain some, er, *interesting* wiring techniques. This book is not intended to turn you into a professional electrician. If you run into questions or problems not addressed here, don't hesitate to **call in an expert** to help. Consider it one more small investment in your home-repair education. If you show an interest, even the busiest contractor will probably take a few minutes to explain what he's doing so you'll know for the next time.

Also call in an expert:

- If you believe a repair has been made correctly but the circuit breaker keeps tripping; or

- If you detect signs of electrical fire or shorting inside a box (the wire's insulation appears blackened or sooty; there are "flash marks" indicating a short to a metal box, etc.)

These rules of thumb, of course, aren't written in stone. In some old houses, ALL the wires are black. You may run into a red wire when you're dealing with a three-way switch, or a blue wire on a ceiling fan. A white wire occasionally is pressed into service as a hot wire to or from a switch (although it SHOULD have been re-coded with black tape by the original installer). And some creative souls have been known to use wires all the colors of the rainbow when they wire their own homes, to allow

---

Identifying The Circuits In Your Electrical Box

Got a helper handy? Grab a small plug-in appliance (radio, lamp, even a power tool) and a waterproof marker. Then turn on all the switches in the house, including bathroom lights and exhaust fans.

Flip the circuit breakers (or unscrew the fuses) one by one, and have your helper tell you which lights go out. Typically, you'll find that one, two, or even three rooms of lights will be controlled by the same circuit. Make a note beside the breaker or inside the panel cover to identify the circuit. (For example, "main & east bedroom lights" or "downstairs bath light & fan.")

Once all the light circuits have been accounted for, flip the remaining breakers off one by one, and have your helper check to see which outlets are "dead" by plugging in the radio or other small appliance. Again, be sure to jot down a few key words such as "kitchen outlets" or "master BR outlets" to help you identify each breaker later.

Remaining breakers (if any) are likely to control major appliance circuits. Flip them off one by one, and have your helper check the dishwasher, refrigerator, washer/dryer, air conditioning unit, etc.

Just as a precaution, it's not a bad idea to confirm that your main breaker is operating properly. Flip all the individual breakers to "on," and then switch the main breaker to "off." Check to make sure that the power is really off – all interior lights, appliances and outlets should NOT be working. (When you're done, of course, flip the main breaker back to "on" – and get your assistant to help you re-set all of your clocks!)

If the main breaker is not already clearly marked, DO SO. Make sure every adult in your household knows where the main breaker is located and how to turn it off in an emergency.

---

them to trace any future wiring problems more easily. But by and large, if you simply remember that black is hot, white is neutral, and green is ground, you'll have it licked.

There you have it — that's all you'll need to know to successfully complete the basic household electrical projects that follow. Ready to tackle a switch, outlet or lamp repair?

Replacing Switches

Wall switches rarely go bad. But perhaps your apartment contains the Murphy's Law exception to that rule. Maybe you're intrigued by the newer switches that glow — a handy way to eliminate fumbling in the dark. Or perhaps you'd simply like to update your decor with those classy, easy-to-use-when-your-hands-are-full rocker switches.

Replacing a wall switch is a great place to begin honing your new electrical skills (not to mention a terrific way to impress friends and family!)

The principle here is simple. The black (hot) wire, as you'll remember, brings power to the outlet or appliance — in this case, the light fixture. The wall switch allows you to interrupt the flow of power by breaking a connection in the black wire. Presto: no power, no light.

Note: In the discussion that follows, we're assuming that you will be replacing a simple switch that is the ONLY control for a particular light. Three-way switches, which allow you to flip a light on and off from two different locations, are quite a bit more complex. Leave those for an expert to tackle, or wait until you've got more electrical experience under your belt.

Here are the tools & materials you'll need to get started:

new single-pole switch
electrical tester
screwdrivers (Phillips & flat-blade)
needlenose pliers
wire cutters
wire strippers

Regular Switch

1. TURN OFF POWER to the switch by flipping the appropriate breaker (or disconnecting the fuse).

2. Remove the two screws (top and bottom) holding the switchplate cover in place. (Drop the screws into a cup or bowl for safe-keeping!)

3. The switch itself will have two screws on the side. CHECK that the power is really off by placing one tip of your electrical tester on one screw and the other on the metal bracket that holds the switch to the wall. Flip the switch on and off. The test light should remain off. Now move the tip of the tester to the other screw, and again flip the switch. No power? Okay. We're ready to remove the old switch.

4. Unscrew the two screws (top and bottom) holding the switch in the box. (Screws loosen by turning counterclockwise, and tighten clockwise.) Tug gently on the switch itself to pull it out of the box, so that you can access the two screws on its side.

5. In most cases, the two wires you see attached to the old switch will be black. That's what the switch does — it interrupts the black (hot) feed, right? Occasionally, an old switch will also have a ground wire attached (usually a bare copper wire). *Note:* On rare occasions, you may find that one of the wires attached to the switch is white but has been re-coded black by the original installer by wrapping a little black tape toward the end. We won't get into the reasons for this here, except to say that the white wire is being pressed into service because a second black wire wasn't available in the commercial cable configuration.

There will most likely be other wires in the box that are NOT attached to the switch. You will probably see two or more white wires joined with a wire nut and may see a bare (ground) wire not attached to anything. The good news is you can IGNORE any wire(s) not attached to your old switch.

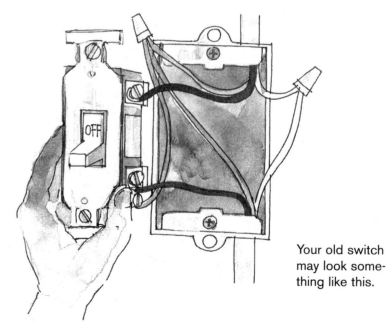

Your old switch may look something like this.

Attach the black wires under the screws of your new switch. Note how the switch bridges the black (hot) wire circuit.

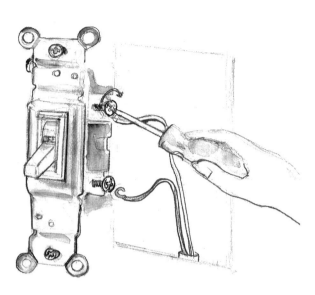

Use wire strippers to remove the insulation from the end of a wire.

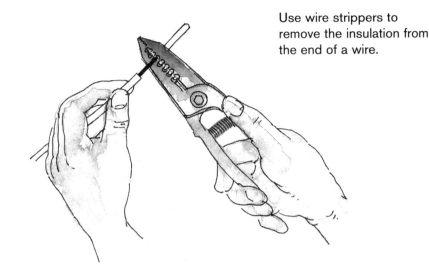

6. Unscrew the screws on the side of the old switch and detach the wires with your needlenose pliers. Then loosen the screws on the NEW switch and re-attach. (If the bare wire ends are badly twisted or scored, cut them off and strip back the insulation with your wire strippers to expose a fresh stretch of bare wire — about 5/8 of an inch should do it.)

It does not matter which black wire goes under the top screw and which goes under the bottom screw — either way, the flow will be interrupted.

Note: In rare cases you may find MORE than one black wire hooked under a contact screw. If so, these wires will need to stay together when you re-attach them to the new switch. See directions on page 8 for making a pigtail.

Most newer switches are not grounded. If your old switch was grounded but your new switch does not provide a green grounding screw, make sure all ground wires in the box are "tied" (twisted together so they make a good connection) and then simply tuck the loose end back into the box.

Switches that light up MAY need to be grounded. Check the package instructions and look for a green grounding screw on the switch. If your old switch was not grounded, look to see if there is a ground wire (typically bare copper) tucked into the box that you can attach to the switch. If not, see instructions below for grounding an outlet (steps 7 and 8 in Replacing an Outlet on page 11).

7. Now gently push the switch back inside the electrical box, making sure it's right side up (!). Screw in the top and bottom mounting screws, and (before you put the switchplate cover back on) restore the power and flip the switch. Lights working? You did it! Screw on the switchplate cover and go brag a little.

Deader than a doornail? Retrace your steps... Turn the power back off, re-check the tightness of the screws, and make sure you haven't inadvertently disconnected or loosened any of the other connections inside the box. Then test again.

Attaching Wires

It looks simple enough, but there IS a right way and a wrong way to attach a wire under a connecting (aka terminal) screw.

Leave just enough bare wire to make about a three-quarter loop around the base of the screw. (Loop the end *clockwise,* so that tightening the screw will tend to tighten rather than loosen the loop.) The wire loop should not cross itself and there should not be exposed wire extending out beyond the screw.

Only one wire should be attached under a terminal screw. Yes, you may find cases where someone else has crammed in two, but that's not the RIGHT way to do it. If two or more wires need to be connected under a single screw, make a "pigtail" — twist the wires together with a short (4-inch to 6-inch) length of similarly sized wire, cap with a wire nut, and then attach only the stripped end of the new addition to the terminal screw.

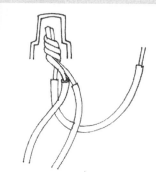

Twist wires together to make a "pigtail."

Tighten the screw down on the wire loop so that it is held snugly in place. Jiggle the wire to make sure; it should not rotate on the screw.

If a box is a tight fit and you find yourself struggling to get the new switch or outlet into its proper spot, it's a good idea to check and retighten screw connections before final installation.

Note: Some switches and outlets now offer "plug-in" connections. Ideally, these allow you to just insert the stripped wire end into a spring-gripped slot, avoiding the need for a terminal screw. In my experience, however, this type of connection is more apt to come undone than the old-fashioned screw-type.

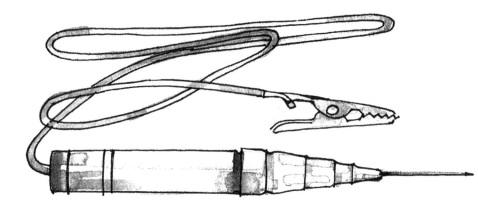

Continuity (electrical) tester

Using An Electrical Tester

Run, don't walk, to your local hardware store if you don't already own an electrical tester (also known as a "continuity tester"). For less than twenty dollars, it's a priceless investment in your own safety and peace of mind.

Simple testers consist of two plastic-coated probes (or one probe and one clip) connected by a short length of wire, with a little window in the handle that will light up when a current is detected.

Worried that a wire might be hot? Place the point of one probe on the wire's bare metal end, and hold the tip of the other probe on a grounded surface (a metal electrical box, bare ground wire, etc.) Then watch the little window in the tester handle. If the light goes on, there's power going through the probe.

You can also use a tester to determine whether you've got power in an outlet. Hold one probe in the round grounding opening and CAREFULLY insert the other probe into the outlet slots, one at a time. (Be careful not to let your fingers touch the bare metal!) Watch for the tell-tale light.

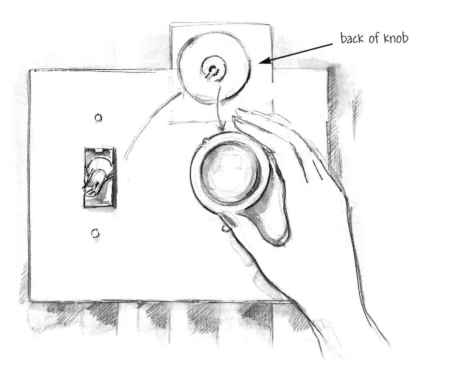

back of knob

Add the dimmer switch knob after the switchplate cover is in place.

Dimmer Switch

Replacing an ordinary wall switch with a dimmer requires almost exactly the same technique as we've just described above for an ordinary single-pole switch. Instead of a switch protruding from the unit, however, you'll have a metal spindle. The dimmer knob pops on AFTER you've installed the switchplate cover. (Check the back of the knob carefully to line it up with any special grooves or flat spots on the spindle.)

Some dimmer switches may be significantly larger than the original switch you are replacing. While they're all designed to fit inside standard electrical boxes, it can be a tight fit if there

is a lot of wire in your box. If you can't seem to get everything tucked back inside the box, ask a knowledgeable friend or electrician to help — you may be able to streamline the connections and do away with some excess wire.

⚠ CAUTIONS & CAVEATS:

- DON'T try to install a dimmer switch in place of a three-way switch (this can be done using a special type of dimmer, but this is a task best left to an expert).

- DON'T install a dimmer to control standard fluorescent fixtures (fluorescents need a special ballast to work with a dimmer control).

- CHECK WITH YOUR CEILING FAN'S MANUFACTURER before installing a dimmer to control the speed of a ceiling fan — you can burn out the fan's motor if it hasn't been designed to handle a variable power supply.

Replacing an Outlet

Got an outlet you think is faulty? Before you decide to replace it, check to be sure you haven't simply popped the breaker. If the breakers look fine and all the other nearby outlets seem to be working, look around for a switch whose function you haven't yet determined — are you sure you're not dealing with a switched outlet? (Don't laugh! I've known folks who called an electrician because they'd never seen such an arrangement before! Naturally, the outlet worked fine as soon as he flipped the switch...)

Another common reason for replacing outlets is to get rid of the old, two-prong type and add the newer three-prong type to accommodate grounded appliances.

Ready to tackle replacing that outlet?

Here are the tools & materials you'll need to get started:

new outlet (preferably 3-prong/grounding type)
electrical tester
screwdrivers (Phillips and flat-blade)
needlenose pliers
wire cutters
wire strippers

If you are replacing an older, two-pronged outlet, you may also need to ground the new outlet using a length of Number 12 bare wire, a drill with a metal 1/8-inch bit, and an assortment of self-tapping green grounding screws. (Just ask your local hardware clerk — they should know exactly what you mean.) Wire is available by the foot at your local hardware store. Some stores also carry pre-cut pieces of green-coated wire especially for grounding purposes.

l. TURN POWER OFF at the panel. Remove the outlet cover by unscrewing the small screw in the center of the cover. CHECK to be sure the power is really off by touching one probe of the electrical tester to one of the screws on the SIDE of the outlet, and the other probe to a grounded surface such as a metal outlet box or mounting bracket. Move the probe to the other screw and check there as well before continuing.

2. Unscrew the two screws (top and bottom) holding the outlet into the box. Gently pull the outlet out of the box so that you can see the four screws on its sides.

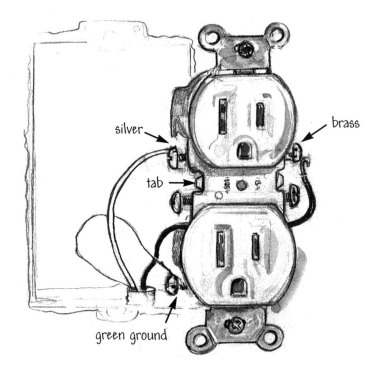

silver — brass

tab →

green ground

Outlets require a ground wire.

3. Take a good look at the way the old outlet is wired. You will notice that the black (hot) wires attach to the pair of dark or brass-colored screws, while the white (neutral) wires connect to the pair of silver or light-colored screws. You may or may not have a (bare) ground wire attached to the bottom of the old outlet.

> **⚠ CAUTIONS & CAVEATS:**
> • NEVER attempt to make a grounded appliance fit a two-pronged outlet by breaking or cutting off the third prong!

There may be other wires in the box too. If they are NOT attached to the outlet, you can disregard them; just make sure you do not dislodge any connections as you work.

4. Pull out your new outlet and take a look at its screw configuration. Again, you will see a pair of screws on one side that are dark, a pair on the other side that are light, and one smaller screw (on the bottom) which is green for — you've got it! — the ground wire. Notice also that there is a small metal tab that connects the sets of screws on both sides. This provides continuity if you are attaching more than one hot or more than one neutral wire. (You will need to break off the tab only if one of the two outlets is separately switched.)

5. Disconnect the black wire from the old outlet and connect it to one of the brass or dark-colored screws on the new outlet. (If there are two black wires, attach each under its own dark-colored screw.) Then move the white wire(s), re-attaching to the silver-colored screw(s) on the new outlet.

6. If a grounding wire is already present (as should be the case if you have a plastic box), disconnect it from the old outlet and re-attach under the green screw of the new outlet.

7. If the old outlet does NOT have a ground wire, you'll need to make one. Cut a six-inch length of Number 12 wire, or select one of the pre-cut green grounding wires. The goal is to attach the new ground wire to the inside of the outlet's metal electrical box.

If you do not have a METAL electrical box AND there is no bare ground wire present, STOP and **call in an expert!**

8. Take a good look at the inside of the metal box. Is there already a green screw to which you could attach the ground wire? How about an existing hole that fits your self-tapping ground screw?

If there isn't a screw or hole available already, you'll need to drill a small hole in the metal box (being careful, of course, not to damage any of the wires in the box) and insert a grounding screw. This is, I will admit, another of those "easier said than done" jobs. It takes a bit of hand strength on the screwdriver to force the screw to tap its way into the metal. Conjure up the image of that nasty driver you encountered on the freeway, get your dander up, and PUSH!

9. Using your needlenose pliers, wrap one bare end of your new ground wire around the grounding screw in the box, and then tighten the screw with a screwdriver to make a snug metal-to-metal connection. Then wrap the other end of the ground wire around the green grounding screw on the bottom of your new outlet, and tighten.

10. As gently as possible, ease the new outlet back into place inside the box. You may need to use your needlenose pliers to bend the wires (carefully!) out of the way. (The convention is to position the outlet's rounded grounding hole at the *bottom* of the three-prong configuration.)

11. Re-check the tightness of your screw connections. Then screw in the two mounting screws (top and bottom) to hold the new outlet in the box, and replace the cover.

12. Turn the power back on and test it by plugging in an appliance. Does it work? You did it!

If you still have a problem, take the cover plate back off and CAREFULLY use your tester to make sure that you have power coming INTO the box through the black wire (holding the probe where it's insulated, touch one end of the tester to the terminal screw holding the black wire and the other to the ground screw or to the screw holding the white wire). Remember, you're expecting power to be present, so be extra careful not to touch a screw, wire or the metal probe end with your fingers.

No power coming through the black wire may mean a circuit breaker has tripped. If there IS power to the box but the outlet isn't working, re-check your connections (turn the power OFF again, first!). Very VERY rarely, a new outlet itself may be defective.

Basic Lighting Projects

Tired of trying to put on your make-up in the dim glow of a one-bulb bathroom? Anxious to pitch that cheapo dining room chandelier — the one you've hated since you moved in?

New light fixtures can be an easy and often inexpensive way to brighten and update your home.

Light fixtures run the gamut of sizes, shapes and designs, and nearly every fixture mounts in a slightly different way. Some fixtures require a mounting bracket and/or a threaded length of tubing called a nipple. Others screw directly to the box. The electrical boxes they are mounted to can also differ in size and shape.

Here are the tools & materials you'll need to get started:

**ladder
replacement fixture
wire nuts (yellow)
goggles (if working on overhead fixture)
electrical tester
screwdrivers (Phillips & flat blade)
wire strippers
wire cutters
needlenose pliers**

Despite all the possible variations on a theme, for the most part the mechanics of installing and removing fixtures tend to be fairly obvious, although sometimes it may take a few minutes of head-scratching.

From an electrical point of view, what goes on inside the light fixture is also pretty simple. The black (hot) wire brings the power in, while the white (neutral) wire provides the "flow" out. Many (but not all) fixtures also contain a ground wire as a safety precaution. A switch which interrupts the hot wire turns the light on and off.

Replacing a Light Fixture

1. TURN POWER OFF at the electrical panel. Remove any globe or diffuser, and save any still-usable light bulbs for future use. (Typically, there are 3 or 4 screws holding a globe in place, while diffusers are secured by a small round cap nut.)

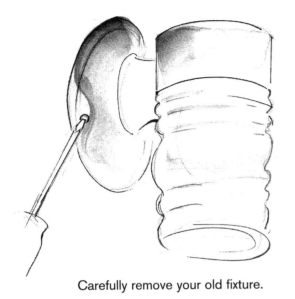

Carefully remove your old fixture.

Additional wires may also be present. If these are joined to the existing fixture's wires, you will need to reconnect them in the same configuration with the black and white wires of the new fixture.

5. Remove the wire nuts, keeping any "grouped" ceiling wires together. Discard the old fixture.

6. Read the mounting instructions for the new fixture. It may or may not mount in exactly the same way as the fixture you just took down, but manufacturers generally include all the parts (mounting straps, nipples, etc.) that you will need to attach the light to your box.

2. Most fixtures will have two screws holding them to the electrical box. (If your fixture has a center nipple poking through, it may be mounted instead by a locknut attached to the center nipple.) Undo the screws or locknut, and the fixture should drop away from the wall or ceiling. (These are often LONG screws!) Support the fixture with one hand or enlist a helper — do NOT allow it to dangle by the wires.

3. Use your electrical tester just to double-check that there is no power to the fixture. (You may need to flip the wall switch on before you test; then be sure to switch it off again.)

4. Study the existing wiring arrangement CAREFULLY. Typically, you will find a white wire from inside the wall or ceiling connecting to the white wire on the old fixture with a wire nut. Similarly, a pair of black wires will be joined by a wire nut. There may also be a bare ground wire attached to the box and (occasionally) to the old fixture.

 **CAUTIONS & CAVEATS:**

- Before working on any type of light fixture, be sure to turn off the power at the electrical panel. Do NOT simply leave the switch turned off. (Depending upon how the fixture has been wired, there may be power to the box even when the switch is in the "off" position.) You've heard it a million times, but it's better to be safe than sorry.

- Don't let fixtures dangle from their wires. Enlist a helper to support the fixture while you work.

- When working on overhead fixtures, wear goggles to protect your eyes from particles of dirt and ceiling material that may drop out.

- Before trying to install any particularly heavy light fixture (a huge wrought-iron chandelier, for example), make sure the existing electrical box is strong enough to safely support it. See the discussion in the section following about Ceiling Fans.

Using Wire Nuts

Yes, I know – they look nothing like the nuts you put out for the holidays. (The "nut" part of the name actually comes from the fact that they are threaded inside, like the nuts that screw onto a bolt.)

Wire nuts are a quick and simple way to connect two or more wires. Just twist the wires together, screw on a wire nut, and – presto! A neat, tidy connection.

But just because it's easy doesn't mean there's any excuse for being sloppy. Choose a good wire nut – make sure it has metal inside, which will not only improve the grip but add its own conductivity to ensure a good connection. (Often the "cheapies" that come with light fixtures and ceiling fans are plain, un-lined plastic – toss them out and use your own!)

Then start with a good, secure connection – make sure you've twisted the wires together TIGHTLY enough to hold on their own, before adding the wire nut. Snip the ends, if necessary, so that only about 1/2 inch of bare wire is showing.

Choose a wire nut big enough to accommodate all the wires you want to join, but small enough that you feel a "bite" as you screw it on. (As a general rule of thumb, a yellow wire nut will join two or three Number 14 wires or two Number 12 wires; use a red wire nut if you need to accommodate bigger assortments than that. If even a red wire nut is too small, they do make bigger ones – but perhaps you are trying to join too many wires at one time. Time to **consult an expert!**)

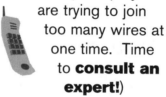

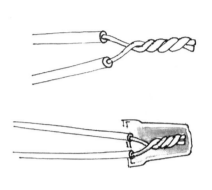

Twist wires together tightly, then cap with a wire nut.

Screw the wire nut on in the same direction as your wires are twisted, so that you're tightening rather than loosening the connection. When you're done, the skirt of the wire nut should completely cover all bare wire to prevent accidental shorts.

Tug gently on the wire nut and each of the individual wires to confirm that the connection is secure.

7. Twist the white wire from your new fixture together with the white wire(s) from the wall or ceiling; screw on a wire nut to hold the bundle tightly together. Do the same for the black wires.

Note: Often the fixture wires will be stranded wire — not easy to twist together securely with the solid wire you find in most household wiring. Strip both wires to expose 3/4 of an inch or so of bare wire, then wrap the stranded wire around the solid conductor as tightly as you can. Twist on a wire nut and tug (GENTLY!) on one wire at a time to be sure you've really got a good connection.

8. If your new fixture comes with a grounding wire, connect the wire to a grounding screw on the box or to a bare ground wire, if one is present.

9. Carefully tuck the wires up inside the fixture, and mount it to the box according to the manufacturer's instructions.

Outside Security Lights

Upgrading an existing outdoor light fixture can provide brighter, more secure lighting around your home. Many of the newer models use halogen bulbs for better illumination. Some contain photosensitive switches that automatically turn lights on at dusk and off at dawn. Others contain an "electric eye" to deter prowlers by snapping on the lights if any movement interrupts the beam.

Spend a little time scouting the aisles of your local hardware outlet or lighting store until you find a product with the features that best suit your needs. Make certain the unit you choose is UL-approved (an electrical device that has met the Underwriter's Laboratory safety standards) and rated for outdoor use.

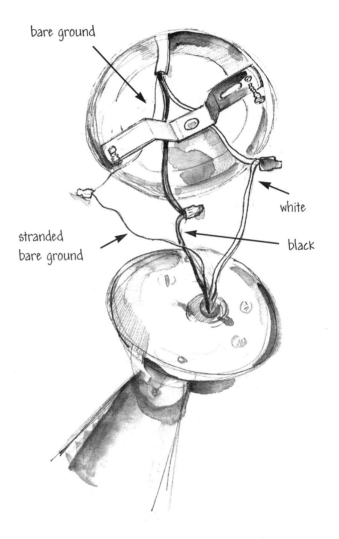

Connect the wires to your new fixture.

To Replace an Existing Exterior Light Fixture

1. TURN OFF POWER at the main breaker.

2. Loosen the existing fixture. (Most wall-mounted exterior lights are fastened with either a pair of screws through the base plate, or a round cap nut near the middle of the fixture that attaches to a short, threaded nipple.) Don't let the fixture dangle by the wires — get a helper to assist you.

3. Get out your tester, flip the light switch on, and DOUBLE-CHECK that there is no power to the fixture. Flip the light switch off again.

4. Disconnect the wire nuts and remove the old fixture wires, making sure you keep any other wires that are joined by each wire nut in their original groupings.

5. Follow the manufacturer's instructions for mounting your new fixture. In general, you will simply join the black wire from the new fixture to the existing black wires, the white wire to the existing whites, and then cap with wire nuts. Ground the fixture to an existing ground wire or to the metal box. (These steps are described in greater detail in the Basic Lighting Projects section above.)

6. Restore power and test the fixture. (If you have chosen a model with an electric eye, you may need to cover the sensor with a piece of heavy tape and wait a minute or two before the lights will turn on.)

Note: It is possible, of course, to add security lights even at locations that don't contain an existing fixture — but it's a MUCH bigger project. Consult an electrician to help you install a new electrical box and extend your wiring to the desired location. Once the new box and wiring are in place, you can install the new light fixture using the steps above.

Re-Wiring a Lamp

Got a favorite old lamp that seems to be on the fritz? Always check the obvious before you decide it's re-wiring time: Is the bulb (ahem) burned out? How about the outlet it's plugged into — are you sure that's working properly? Plug in another appliance that you KNOW is working, just to be certain.

Once you've ruled out such obvious sources of trouble, unplug the lamp and take a close look at its cord and plug. Are there any spots where the insulation is nicked, damaged or frayed? Is the cord/plug connection wobbly or coming apart? Do the plug prongs look broken or worn? If there's an obvious problem with the plug or cord, that's probably all you'll need to replace.

If the cord and plug look okay, the trouble probably lies in the lamp's socket or switch. (In many but not all lamps, the switch and socket are combined in one compact unit, which makes it especially simple to replace both.)

Here are the tools & materials you'll need to get started:

screwdrivers (Phillips and flat-blade)
wire cutters
wire stripper
razor knife

1. MAKE SURE THE LAMP IS UNPLUGGED. Remove the shade and bulb.

2. The curved metal bracket that holds the shade is known as a "harp." Detach the harp from its bracket. (You may need to pull up on a small locking sleeve or unscrew a nut holding each end of the harp, and then pinch the ends inward to release them from the bracket.)

3. Take a close look at the socket's metal housing — you'll see that it consists of two pieces, crimped together. Disassemble by pushing inward on the sides of the smaller piece, right where they join. (The word "press" may be stamped into the metal.)

4. The outer (metal) housing will come off, followed by a cardboard insulating sleeve. What's left is the socket and switch itself — with the lamp cord wires attached by screws on the sides or bottom of the unit.

5. You can unscrew the screws and untie the "UL knot" (the same half-knot you use to tie your shoelaces) at the base of the socket, or (if you plan on replacing the socket as well as the cord) simply snip the wires. (You DID unplug the lamp before we began, right?)

> **TIP:**
> Consider replacing an ordinary light socket with a 3-way socket for greater versatility. If you do, however, some experts suggest you use a slightly heavier cord. Ask your hardware salesperson to help you select the right combination.

6. If you're replacing the socket, take the old socket WITH you to your local hardware store, just to make sure you buy the correct replacement unit. If the cord needs to be replaced, it's a good idea to bring a small section of the original

> **TIP:**
> If you're worried that it might be difficult to feed the new wire into place inside the lamp, BEFORE YOU REMOVE THE OLD CORD splice it to the new one to pull it easily into place. (If you've purchased a cord with plug attached, cut the plug off your old cord and splice it to the new cord at the BOTTOM of the lamp; then pull the new cord through.)

cord AND to jot down its approximate original length. Don't forget to also purchase a plug (preferably one that's polarized) if your new cord doesn't already come with plug attached.

7. Reassemble, making sure you include the "UL knot" before attaching the wires to the terminal screws, to help protect the connections from accidental tugs.

A Variation on the Theme

Some lamps have a separate switch located in the base of the lamp. If replacing the socket doesn't seem to help, the problem may be in the switch. Make sure the lamp is unplugged, then remove the switch by unscrewing the locknut that holds the switch to the base. Ask your hardware salesman to help you find an exact replacement.

Hanging a Ceiling Fan

Ceiling fans not only add that inviting *Casablanca* look to your home or apartment, they're also an investment in energy efficiency. The reversible motors available on most ceiling fans allow you to switch from a cooling down-draft in summer to an opposite rotation that creates an up-draft to circulate warmer air back into the room during winter months.

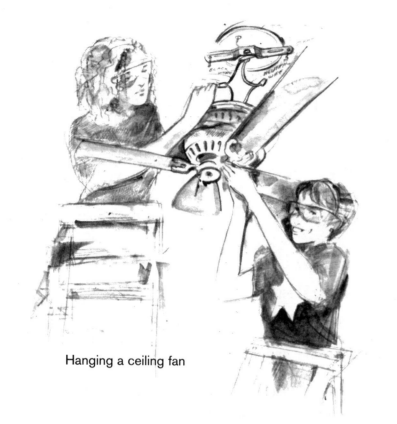

Hanging a ceiling fan

So before you rush out and purchase that deluxe, super-air-moving model with the hand-woven rattan trim, take a minute to investigate what's up there in the ceiling to support it.

Checking Out Your Ceiling Support

Here are the tools & materials you'll need to get started:

ladder (preferably 2)
goggles
screwdrivers
electrical tester
yellow wire nuts
a helper

1. TURN POWER OFF to your existing overhead light fixture at the main breaker (NOT just the wall switch!)

2. Don a pair of goggles to protect your eyes. There's nothing worse than having a piece of ceiling plaster land squarely in your eye while you're trying to maintain your balance atop a ladder.

3. Speaking of ladders, make sure you're using one tall enough for the job. Tottering atop a tiny step-stool or milk crate is NOT a safe way to go.

4. Have a helper standing by (preferably on her own ladder), while you remove the globe and bulb from your existing fixture. Then loosen the cap nut or screws holding the fixture to the ceiling. Let your helper support the fixture so that it doesn't dangle by its wiring.

Hanging a new ceiling fan in place of an existing overhead light fixture sounds like it should be a relatively simple project. And many times it is. Just make sure that the location allows enough side-to-side room for the blades to turn properly, and that you'll be leaving ample headroom below the fixture (7 feet is a minimum).

The big question, however, is whether the electrical box in your ceiling is mounted securely enough to support the substantial weight of a ceiling fan's motor.

Ladder Safety

You know that old superstition about the "bad luck" produced by walking under a ladder? Well, it doesn't take a crystal ball to figure out where such common wisdom originated. Ladders are great tools, but they do deserve to be used with respect. Here are a few basic safety tips:

• Use the right tool for the job. Don't teeter on a milk crate or atop a 5-gallon bucket, even for a task that'll "just take a minute" — take the time to fetch a sturdy step-stool or ladder.

• For electrical jobs, choose a wooden or fiberglass ladder rather than an aluminum one.

• Before you start to climb, always check to make sure the bracing arms of a step-ladder or the extension latches on a telescoping ladder are fully locked, and that the feet are resting securely on a flat surface.

• Don't try to stand on the top rung or two — if you need a higher reach, get a taller ladder. And remember that the flip-out tool shelf on a stepladder is just that. It's designed to hold tools and paint buckets, not humans.

• Teach the smaller members of your household to give a wide berth to anyone working on a ladder. A dropped tool or upended paint bucket could spell disaster.

5. Use the electrical tester to make SURE all power is off to the ceiling box. Flip the wall switch on and check again. Then turn the wall switch back off.

6. Inspect the ceiling box itself. (You may need to gently pull some additional wires down out of the box so you can see — be careful not to detach any of the connections as you do so!)

Is the box made of metal or plastic? Is it mounted directly up through the box to a ceiling joist, or does it appear to be mounted on one side only? Is it solidly in place, or can you wiggle it a little?

Ideally, your box will be a metal "pancake box" screwed directly to the wooden ceiling joist above it. Pancake boxes, like their name, are round and relatively flat — typically less than an inch in depth. If your ceiling contains a metal pancake box and it seems to be firmly anchored in place, chances are it should support a normal-sized ceiling fan (35 to 40 pounds) with no problem.

Another common type of electrical box is a hexagonal-shaped metal box with a flange on one end that is mounted sideways to the ceiling joist. The flange, of course, will be hidden from view inside the ceiling, but you may be able to see wood through little holes in one side of the box. Depending upon how securely the flange is mounted to the joist and how heavy a ceiling fan you plan to hang, this type of box may or may not support the fan. If there's any question in your mind, **call in an expert** for advice.

TIP:

Now is a good time to inspect the visible portion of your house wires. If the insulation appears cracked or frayed, you may want to reinforce it with a good wrapping of electrical tape. Electrical tape comes in a variety of colors. Be sure you use the appropriate color tape to properly identify the wires OR tag them in some other way for future reference. If you don't have white tape handy to identify white (neutral) wires, for example, you can reinforce the wire with black electrician's tape and then add a strip of white bandage-type tape.

In newer homes and apartments, chances are your ceiling box will be plastic rather than metal. These plastic boxes are typically NOT adequately supported to safely accommodate a ceiling fan's weight.

Ceiling box not up to the job, but you can't get that gorgeous fan out of your mind? All's not lost. It IS possible in most cases either to reinforce the existing box or to replace it with a properly-supported substitute. But it takes some doing. There are several types of ceiling fan support kits on the market — check with your local hardware store for a closer look. Most either require you to crawl up in the attic to brace the box between two ceiling joists, or to insert bracing rods through a 4 1/2-inch hole in the ceiling. Easier said than done, of course. This is probably a job to leave to someone with experience.

Installing the Ceiling Fan

Once you've made sure your ceiling box will support the fan of your dreams, the actual installation of a new ceiling fan is fairly straightforward.

1. Power still off? Go ahead and unscrew the wire nuts connecting the house wires to the old fixture, being careful to note the configuration of any wires that may be joined — keep grouped wires together. Discard the old fixture.

2. Follow the instructions that came with your new ceiling fan. Generally, you will first attach a mounting bracket to the ceiling box (which is the reason we were so concerned that the box would support the weight!).

3. With some models, you may have to decide at this point

Clockwise or Counterclockwise? That Is The Question!

Which direction should your ceiling fan turn? Some manufacturers' instructions talk about "forward" or "reverse" for warm- and cool-weather operation. But which direction is which?? The brochures don't always specify.

To make things even more confusing, terms like "clockwise" and "counterclockwise" are relative. A fan that's spinning clockwise if you're looking DOWN on it is actually rotating counterclockwise if you're standing underneath looking UP.

Frankly, the direction of a fan's rotation doesn't make THAT much of a difference — whichever way it goes it will circulate the air in a room, helping to equalize the temperature. But here are a few quick tips for remembering which direction is which.

- When the trailing edge of the blade is down, the fan is pushing air down into the room, creating a cooling breeze for hot weather. Generally (though I hesitate to say always), this direction will be counterclockwise, viewed from the floor and looking up.

- If, on the other hand, the leading edge of the fan is down (a clockwise rotation), the fan will be scooping room air upwards, helping to warm the house in winter.

- And, of course, the simplest test of all: stand a safe distance from the fan and see if you can feel a downward breeze.

whether you want to mount the fan close to the ceiling, or whether you want to use the "down rod." A higher fixture obviously will provide better clearance, but having the fan blades a bit lower will do a better job of circulating the air. Remember, you'll need to leave at least 7 feet of clearance for safety.

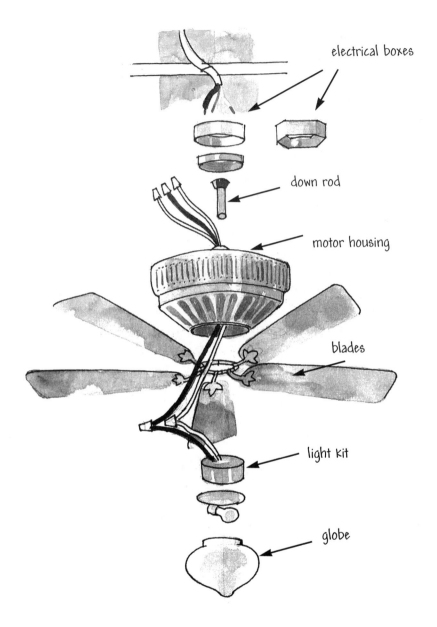

electrical boxes

down rod

motor housing

blades

light kit

globe

Ceiling fan components may vary slightly, depending on the manufacturer. Some light kits come pre-wired or with snap-together connections.

4. Once the mounting bracket and down rod (if any) are securely locked in place, have a helper support the motor or suspend it from the bracket according to package instructions. (A specially designed hook comes with some models). Then connect the fan's wiring to the house wiring — in most cases, that will be a simple matter of black to black, white to white, and ground to ground. If your ceiling fan comes with a light kit, you may also have an additional hot wire (typically blue) to feed power to the lights. Join the blue wire to the blacks. (Some newer fans make it even easier by providing snap-together wiring connections!)

> **TIP:**
> The hardware that comes with some fan kits may not include the necessary wire nuts, or they may throw in the cheap kind which do not have metal threads inside. Use your own good-quality wire nuts to ensure a tight connection.

5. You're almost done now! Again, package directions will vary somewhat, but typically once the wires are connected you will slide a canopy up to cover the wiring and attach it with screws, and then assemble and attach the blades.

6. Turn the power back on and test. (You may need to try various positions for the switch and/or pull-cord on the ceiling fan to get the lights to work via your wall switch and the motor to turn in the direction you want.) Make sure the blades are properly balanced (the instructions that came with your fan should provide particulars) before operating the fan for any length of time.

Got a good breeze going? You did it!

No whiz, buzz or whirr? Most manufacturers include a trouble-shooting section in the instruction manual. If they're especially kind, they may also provide a toll-free number you can call for technical support.

Adding a Telephone Jack

Let's face it — we live in a communications era. The days when a single telephone served an entire household are as passé as "I Like Ike" buttons. Today, we have separate phones for talkative teens; lines for our home-office phone and fax; and more and more frequently, a dedicated Internet connection.

But (particularly in older homes) we don't always have phone jacks where we most need or want them. Luckily, adding a phone jack is one of the easiest do-it-yourself projects.

Here's some basic information before we begin: Telephones operate on a simple two-wire, low-voltage system. That is, only two wires are needed to make the phone operational. In most newer homes, however, the phone company has anticipated that you might someday want to add additional phone lines, and thoughtfully provides six wires (enough to provide three separate phone numbers) in the basic service wire that attaches to your home. (If you have only the older 2-wire service to your home, the phone company will upgrade it to a 6-wire service, usually at no charge, if you order an additional incoming phone line.)

Back in the days when the phone company owned both the service equipment AND the phones and wires inside your home, telephones were "hard-wired" in place. With the advent of deregulation in 1974, consumers got the option to own

their own telephones — but they needed a way to quickly and conveniently remove and change them. The now-ubiquitous modular phone jack was born.

A standard phone line, though versatile, is not infinitely expandable. Most phone companies provide enough power on each line to operate the ringers on about five telephones. (You can add more phones than that to a line, but they may not all ring.) Before you decide to install additional phones, check the "ringer equivalence number" (REN) stamped into the base of the phone or printed on the manufacturer's label. Typically, your phones will be rated at 1.0 or 0.5 REN. If the REN total for all phones in your house adds up to 5 or less, there should be enough power for all the phones to ring.

Consult your local phone company before beginning any work on your phone lines; they *may* have rules or restrictions you should know about before you begin. If you have subscribed to a wiring-maintenance program, for example, tinkering with your own phone wiring inside the house may void their coverage.

Converting a Hard-wired Phone to Modular Jack

This project assumes you have a hard-wired phone (that is, one wired directly into the wall) and that you'd like to replace it with a modular jack and newer plug-in-type telephone.

Here are the tools & materials you'll need to get started:

wire strippers
wire cutters
screwdrivers
modular jack converter
new telephone

CAUTIONS & CAVEATS:

- NEVER attempt to work on any telephone wiring if you wear a pacemaker!!!!

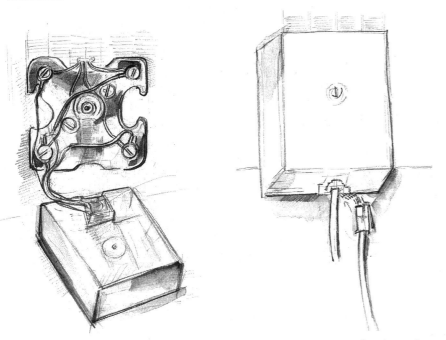

Match the conversion jack's wires with those of your phone line by color.

1. TAKE THE PHONE OFF THE HOOK before you begin. (Although telephones operate on a relatively safe, low-voltage system, the charge coming through the wires increases when an incoming call activates the ringer.)

2. Remove the screw holding the cover of the old (hard-wired) jack in place, and take off the cover. Look carefully at the four terminal screws and note the different colored wires going to each terminal. One set of wires will come from the incoming phone line, and the other will belong to the old (hard-wired) telephone itself.

3. Clip off the wires belonging to the telephone ONLY. (Do NOT cut the wires from the incoming phone line.)

4. The new modular jack converter may attach in one of several possible ways. It may require you to loosen the terminal screws and insert "spade connectors" (U-shaped metal ends) underneath the screws. Or, it may provide cap connectors that simply snap over the screws. Just be sure to read package instructions carefully, and match up the converter's wire colors with the colors of the existing incoming phone wires.

5. Carefully tuck the wires under the new converter's cover, and secure with the screw provided. Plug in your new phone, and you should be ready to roll! (Don't forget to hang up the handset if you took an extension phone off the hook.)

Installing an Extra Phone Jack

Suppose you already have a modular-type phone jack, but want to install an extension phone in another part of the house. The simplest (although not exactly elegant) solution is to buy a "duplex jack" that plugs into your existing modular receptacle and gives you TWO places to plug in phones. Plug your original phone into one, then run a long extension cord (not in trafficways, please!) to the second phone.

The better solution is to add a junction box and an additional modular jack.

Here are the tools & materials you'll need to get started:

razor knife   drill and 1/4-inch drill bit
wire strippers   hammer
wire cutters   studfinder
screwdrivers   junction box
surface-mount modular jack
telephone cable (buy the 6-conductor type, just in
    case)
insulated cable staples
new telephone

1. BEFORE YOU START, take the phone off the hook. If your phone is the type with a light in it, also look for and unplug any TRANSFORMER supplying power to the phone.

2. Following the manufacturer's instructions, install the junction box near your original phone jack. Basically, the junction box will provide a series of terminal screws to enable you to connect the new cable to an extension wire that plugs into the original phone jack. Just be sure to match colors under the terminal screws.

3. Run the new phone cable to the location where you plan to install the new jack. You can route cable along the baseboard and up and over door molding, if you want the new phone in the same room as the old phone. Staple cable in place (carefully!) using a hammer and cable staples.

If you're running cable from one room to another, DON'T try to run the cable through a door opening. The easiest solution is often to drill a small (1/4-inch) hole through a closet or other common wall. (Use the studfinder to locate studs in the wall, and drill in the open space BETWEEN them.) If you have a crawl space or basement underneath your house, you can also drill down and run the wire that way.

After you've drilled a hole for the cable, use a hooked piece of wire coat-hanger or a plastic drinking straw inserted in the hole as a guide to help you thread the cable through.

4. Once you've got the cable to the location where you'd like the new phone jack, use a razor knife to strip back the outer cable insulation, and then gently strip each of the 6 small wires inside (using wire strippers) to allow about 1/2 inch of bare wire to show.

5. Read the manufacturer's instructions for installing the new phone jack, and connect the wires as shown. (Just be sure to match colors, and you'll be fine.) Typically, the jack unit mounts to the wall with one or two screws. Use a studfinder to locate a wooden stud, or screw the jack to a wooden baseboard.

6. Hang up the off-the-hook receiver, and plug in your new phone. If you don't have a dial tone, retrace your steps and make sure all wires are securely connected under their terminal screws and that like-colored wires are properly matched.

> ⚠ **CAUTIONS & CAVEATS:**
>
> • *Before you drill,* do your best to locate (and avoid) plumbing or electrical wiring inside the wall. Avoid walls that contain plumbing fixtures, and don't drill near an existing electrical outlet. Do NOT run telephone wire in damp locations or close to water pipes, electrical conduit, or sheet metal ductwork.

Chapter 2
PLUMBING PROJECTS

Plumbing Basics

At times I've wondered whether plumbing fixtures aren't really some as-yet-unrecognized sentient life form that KNOWS when the hardware store is closed. It seems whatever can go wrong with plumbing, will — and usually at night, on a weekend, or when you're planning a trip out of town.

Compounding the challenge, plumbing parts have been sadistically designed to all LOOK alike without actually being interchangeable, by engineers who have refused to accept the concept of standardization. So even the simplest plumbing repair can (and usually does) require multiple trips to the hardware store.

That said, let me pass along the four cardinal rules for plumbing survival:

1. Cultivate a good working relationship with a well-stocked hardware store or plumbing supply house. A knowledgeable parts-person is worth his or her weight in gold.

2. Always bring the old plumbing parts with you to the store, along with every scrap of information you can jot down about whatever you CAN'T bring with you (the make and model of your toilet, for example).

3. Don't hastily rip open packages containing new parts; slit them carefully with a razor knife so they can be taped neatly shut if (or more likely, when) you return them.

4. Never, ever throw old parts away until you are POSITIVE you've found a suitable, working replacement.

Stripped to its bare essentials, plumbing is actually a fairly elementary system. A water main feeds water to your house, probably through a meter that allows the utility company to send you those friendly greeting notices from time to time. A shut-off valve is typically located somewhere near the meter box, and another shut-off is generally provided where the water enters your house.

The water line usually splits shortly after entering the house, with one section feeding the hot water heater. Parallel hot and cold water supply lines then feed your sinks, bathtubs, kitchen and laundry. (The one exception is toilets, which of course don't require hot water and are supplied only by a cold-water feed.) Separate shut-off valves are generally provided on each water supply line so that water can be turned off to a particular appliance or fixture without affecting everything else in the house.

That's the supply end of things. Drains, of course, are another major component of a plumbing system. Drains from your sink, toilet, bathtub, etc. connect to waste pipes. And to prevent a build-up of sewer gases and a possible drainage-inhibiting vacuum, waste pipes are vented to the outside air through tall pipes that protrude out the top of your roof.

While working on plumbing can be frustrating, most simple household plumbing repairs just take a bit of common sense and persistence. Before undertaking any major plumbing project, however, be sure to check with your local building department about any special codes and permit requirements.

Demystifying the Innards of a Toilet

The toilet, or so the legend goes, was invented around 1860 by an Englishman with the euphonious name of Thomas A. Crapper. Today we pretty much take these white porcelain edifices for granted. But talk to your mother or grandmother; many still remember cold winter dashes to the outhouse. (And if they're old enough to recall that, they'll probably regale you with tales about trudging to school in the snow as well...)

The Great Crapper Myth

Yes, there really was a Thomas Crapper, but — at least according to a fascinating article in *Plumbing & Mechanical Magazine* — he didn't actually invent the toilet. Mr. Crapper apparently built a, er, name for himself in the toilet business by marketing the "Silent Valveless Water Waste Preventer," a patent issued to another inventor in 1819.

An enterprising gentleman, Crapper owned nine plumbing-related patents, operated two plumbing shops and served as "sanitary engineer" for several members of English royalty. But the popular association with his name may well have come from the doughboys of World War I, who saw the "T. Crapper-Chelsea" trade name emblazoned in English on toilet tanks.

For a fascinating look at this neglected bit of plumbing history, visit:

http://www.theplumber.com/crapper.html

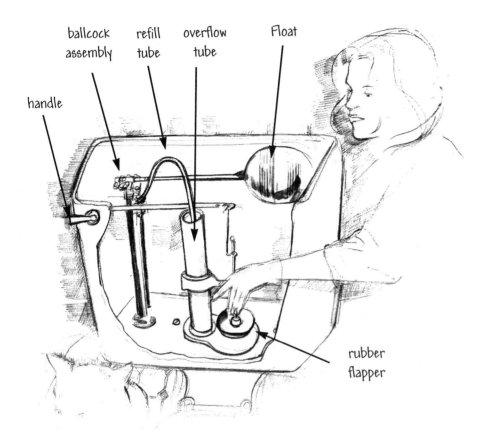

handle

ballcock assembly · refill tube · overflow tube · Float

rubber flapper

- The ballcock assembly, a tall stand-pipe fixture that usually sits to the left inside the tank. When triggered by the float, a valve in the ballcock opens to allow water to fill up the tank.

- The overflow tube, a vertical pipe just to the right of the ballcock assembly, which channels any excess water back into the bowl. Note that a thin piece of tubing leads out of the top of the ballcock assembly and into the overflow tube; this is what refills the toilet bowl after a flush.

- A rubber flapper or ball stopper that sits on the bottom of the tank, below the float which lifts to allow the water in the tank to flush out into the toilet, and

- That all-important trigger mechanism, the flush handle.

So here's what happens when you push down on the handle: The lever attached to the back of the handle pulls the flapper (or in older models, the ball stopper) up and away from its seat, letting the water in the tank flush down into the toilet bowl.

The pressure and downward flow of water from the bowl into the drain creates a siphoning action that helps to empty the toilet bowl.

As the water level in the tank drops, the float rides downward. The pressure on the other end of the float arm opens a valve in the ballcock assembly, so that when the flush is over, water flows back into the tank through the assembly. Water is also sent back through the overflow tube to fill up the toilet bowl again, via the refill tube.

When you first peer under the lid on your toilet tank, the innards can seem to be a bewildering array of balls, levers and chains. But it's really not as complicated as it may seem. Take a quick look now, and see if you can identify the following basic components:

- The float, a round ball that (as its name implies) floats on the surface of the water.

The flapper falls back to seal the outlet opening. Rising water in the tank lifts the float, and when it reaches a certain level, it shuts off the valve in the ballcock.

Note: Some newer ballcock assemblies don't use the old traditional float and float arm; a cup that moves up and down on a stem opens and closes the valve by water pressure.

Toilet Trouble-Shooting

Condensation/Sweating

That icky dampness that accumulates on the outside of your toilet tank is caused by the combination of cold water inside the tank and warmer air in the bathroom. Unless you have EXTREMELY cold incoming water, the solution is pretty simple — insulate the inside of the toilet tank to prevent that cold-to-warm contact.

Ask your friendly neighborhood hardware store for a toilet insulation kit. These inexpensive kits come complete with cut-to-fit polystyrene or styrofoam insulating material plus an appropriate adhesive. You'll need to drain your toilet tank before applying the insulation — turn off the waterstop under your toilet tank, flush, sponge out any excess water, and let the tank dry. Then follow package directions.

Be sure to pick a time when you can let the toilet stand idle for at least 24 hours so the adhesive can dry completely before refilling the tank.

Toilet Keeps Running

Toilets that "run" continually are not only a noisy nuisance, they can also waste a great deal of water (and, if you pay for water via a metered system, money!).

The most common reason for a "running" toilet is a faulty flapper or ball stopper, which is letting water seep past and into the bowl. An easy way to test for "flapper seep" is to pour a dash of food coloring into the tank. Make sure nobody flushes the toilet for a few hours, then check the water in the bowl. If flapper seep is your problem, the colored water will have migrated into the bowl.

To replace the flapper or ball stopper, turn the water off at the waterstop and flush to drain the tank. Sponge out any remaining water and unhook the lift chain. Ball stoppers generally unscrew from the lift wire. Flappers may attach in a variety of ways; you may need to loosen a thumbscrew and slide the flapper assembly up the overflow tube, or simply unhook the arms holding it in place.

If the flapper or ball stopper seems to be in good condition, the problem may simply be corrosion or an accumulation of minerals on the seat where it rests. A gentle buffing with fine steel wool or a non-metallic abrasive pad will often restore the surface so that the flapper or ball stopper will seat more effectively.

With ball stoppers in particular, yet another possible cause for a "running" toilet is an out-of-adjustment linkage. Make sure the lift wires and connecting chain or rod are positioned so that the ball stopper drops straight down onto the seat.

Whistling Toilet

Water leaking through a ballcock assembly valve into the tank can cause a high-pitched whistling or "singing" noise.

To test for a ballcock valve problem, pull up gently on the float. If the noise stops, either the ballcock valve is faulty or (with any luck), you may just need to bend the float arm downward a hair to close the valve sooner.

It IS possible to rebuild the ballcock valve, but (particularly with older models) it often pays to simply replace the entire assembly.

Replacing the Ballcock Assembly

Here are the tools & materials you'll need to get started:

adjustable (crescent) wrench
locking pliers (visegrips)
penetrating oil, if necessary
**replacement ballcock (wait to purchase until you can
    bring the old one with you)**
new toilet water supply line (ditto)

1. Turn off the water at the waterstop; drain the tank by flushing. Sponge out any remaining water. Unhook the small refill tube from the overflow tube, and detach the float arm from the ballcock assembly.

2. Using an adjustable wrench, disconnect the water supply line where it feeds into the outside of the tank.

3. Now the tough part: you'll need to loosen the nut underneath the tank holding the ballcock assembly in place. Work carefully so you don't crack the porcelain. You may need to grip the ballcock shaft (inside the tank) using locking pliers and wedging the pliers against the side of the tank, while you loosen the nut outside with a crescent wrench. If necessary, apply a liberal dose of penetrating oil, and wait (overnight, if possible). When all else fails, plumbers have been known to saw through the outside nut and ballcock shaft with a hacksaw, but this can take time and lots of patience. Be VERY careful not to crack the tank!

4. Take the old ballcock assembly with you to the store. The most fool-proof plan is always to simply replace it with exactly the same model, if you can. You might opt instead for a newer "floating cup" ballcock. These units don't have a separate float arm; you can raise or lower the water level by pinching the clip and moving it up or down the shaft. However, remember that a replacement kit that says "fits most toilets" may or may not actually fit yours! If in doubt, make sure you can return the part if necessary.

5. Before installing the new assembly, carefully clean the inside surface of the tank where the base of the unit will rest, to assure a water-tight connection. Install the assembly according to package directions. Don't forget to clip the new refill tube into the overflow and re-attach the float ball arm.

6. You can just re-attach the old water supply line. But they're so cheap, go ahead and spring for a new one! Consider it a little extra insurance against leaks. (Just make sure you purchase a water supply line for a TOILET, not a faucet).

7. Adjust the water level by bending the float arm (bending the arm up raises the water level; bending it down will decrease it.) In general, the water level should be about half an inch below the top of the overflow tube.

Lazy Flush

A "lazy flush" problem may be caused by mineral build-up in the flush holes located around the rim of the toilet bowl which slow the delivery of water.

Cleaning out these small holes is no easy task; in some cases, the only solution may be replacing the entire toilet. Before you resort to such drastic measures, however, you can try a de-liming treatment. Scrub the bowl well. Turn the water off at the waterstop and flush the toilet to drain the tank. Then sponge out any excess water inside the tank.

Make long rolls of paper towels and anchor them in place up under the rim of the toilet bowl, using plumber's putty to hold them in place. Raise the flapper or stopper ball and pour a commercial lime remover into the tank so that it drains through, soaking the paper towels. Leave the paper towels in place for a full day, if possible. (Lime removers can be caustic; be sure to protect your hands with rubber gloves before removing the paper towels and putty or tape!) Turn the water-stop back on.

Some of the first 1.6-gallon water-saving toilets didn't quite have the hydrodynamic bugs worked out and were notorious for lazy-flush problems. Owners of some of these toilets simply got used to flushing twice, if necessary. Newer toilet designs use pressurized air and larger-diameter openings to overcome the problems with the original water-saving models. After-market "adaptor kits" are also available to retrofit some earlier low-flush units, although reports on their performance are mixed.

Recent posts to plumbing web sites suggest that lazy-flush problems with some of the 1.6-gallon water-saving toilets may be related to use of those drop-in blue tank tablets. Try removing the tablets and flush several times to see if the problem clears up.

Toilet Won't Flush

If your toilet won't flush at all, start with the basics — do you have water in the tank? If the tank is empty, check the linkage between the handle and flapper or ball stopper. The problem is often simply a broken chain, lift wire, or handle.

Occasionally, there may be debris clogging the opening between the tank and bowl. Try gently running a bent coat hanger wire through the opening. If you're not immediately able to dislodge the clog, however, STOP and call a plumber. The problem may require detaching the tank from the bowl or other more extreme intervention.

Tank Won't Fill

Double-check the obvious first — has someone turned the waterstop off without bothering to say anything?

If that's not the problem, it could be that the ballcock valve (which controls the flow of water into the tank) is sticking. Sometimes just jiggling the float arm will be enough to loosen the valve. If that doesn't work or if the problem recurs, replace the ballcock assembly. (See instructions above.)

Toilet Overflows

This most common of toilet woes usually seems to occur just when you are expecting guests.

Plunge GENTLY at first with a plumber's helper/plunger, increasing the pace and energy behind your push a little at a time. If you can't seem to budge the clog after about 50 plunges, try a toilet auger or call a professional. (See the section Using an Auger later in this chapter.)

Leaks

The three most common sources of toilet leaks are at the waterstop itself, at the supply line/tank connection, and around the hold-down bolts that connect the tank to the bowl.

Once you've isolated the source of the leak, you may be able to solve the problem by simply tightening the connection. (For the hold-down bolts, you may need to hold the nut underneath the tank steady with a wrench while tightening the bolt inside the tank with a screwdriver.) Be careful, of course, not to overtighten or you may crack the connecting parts or (worse yet!) the porcelain!

Although it's rare, you MAY encounter a leak around the very base of the toilet, where a wax ring is supposed to seal the connection to the waste pipe. Replacing the wax ring is not a fun job, but it's also not terribly difficult. Empty the toilet of as much water as possible by turning off the water supply line and flushing, then bail out any remaining water. Disconnect the water supply line and unscrew the two bolts (a few models use 4 bolts), holding the toilet to the floor. Carefully pick up the toilet (you may want to enlist a helper here) and move it a few feet away. Using a putty knife, gently scrape away the old wax ring, making sure you also pull out any plastic base attached to the wax. Insert a new wax ring, and reset and reconnect the toilet. Tighten the mounting bolts GENTLY to (once again!) avoid cracking the porcelain.

Leaks, of course, can also result from a crack in the porcelain tank or bowl. Yes, you'll hear heroic stories about various

CAUTIONS & CAVEATS:

Do NOT attempt to clear a toilet clog with liquid drain cleaner or electric snake. The chemicals in liquid drain cleaners are generally more effective on grease-and-hair stoppages than toilet clogs, and some generate heat which can crack or damage the porcelain fixture – just picture THAT mess! Electric snakes are great for clogs further down the waste pipe, but can crack delicate porcelain.

porcelain repairs that lasted for decades. But then again, there are watery tales of woe involving repairs that failed. My advice is to play it safe; consider even a hairline crack a fatal illness for which there is no cure. Go ahead and replace the entire toilet.

Loose Handle

Tightening the toilet handle requires just a gentle twist of a crescent wrench on the locknut inside the tank. The only trick here is that the nuts on most toilet handles thread BACK-WARDS from the way parts normally screw together. So turn clockwise to loosen, counterclockwise to tighten. Many locknuts are made of plastic, so be careful not to overtighten!

Replacing a Shower Head

Want to modernize the look in your bath? Tired of that low-flow shower head that seems to have become a "no-flow" model? Or, on the flip side, looking for an easy and inexpensive way to conserve water?

Changing shower heads is simply a matter of screwing the old one off and screwing the new one on.

Here are the tools & materials you'll need to get started:

adjustable (crescent) wrench (medium size)
small pipe wrench
electrician's or duct tape
teflon tape
small (toothbrush-size) wire brush
**new shower head (if you can't salvage the old one —
      see below)**

1. Fit your crescent wrench to the nut at the base of the shower head itself (where the shower head attaches to the pipe), and turn counterclockwise. (Some conical-style shower heads thread on without an exposed nut — just use your hand to unscrew.) Be careful NOT to turn the water pipe that the shower head attaches to — you don't want to unscrew *that* way back inside the wall! If necessary, wrap tape around the toothed jaws of your pipe wrench to keep from gouging the metal, and grip the water pipe with the pipe wrench to keep it steady as you turn the crescent wrench.

    Note: If your water pipe has a ball on the end after you remove the shower head, you'll have to either replace the shower head with a similar type of fixture OR replace the water pipe with one that has threads at the end.

2. Once you've removed the old shower head, check the condition of the pipe end and threads. Clean off any old tape or crud that's built up in the threads using a small wire brush. If the pipe or threads are badly corroded or if there is a significant mineral build-up constricting the inside of the pipe, consider **calling in an expert.** You may need to replace the pipe from its junction inside the wall or (heaven forbid!), it may be time to consider re-plumbing part or all of your house. (We'll keep our fingers crossed that you never have to deal with *that!*)

> **TIP:**
> Can't get the shower head to budge? Squirt a few drops of penetrating oil at the connection (try to get it into the threads, if possible), and try again in 12 to 24 hours.

3. If the holes in your old shower head seem to be encrusted with mineral build-up, it may be worth trying to resurrect the old part with a good, long soak in a commercial lime remover before you go out and purchase a new one.

    If you've got a water-saver model that makes you feel like you practically have to run around in the shower stall just to get damp, you may be able to fix the problem by removing the flow restrictor — a small plastic cap or wafer that fits inside the shower head. Just unscrew the faceplate (the part where the water comes out), turn the shower head over and poke from the opposite end with a miniature screwdriver until the cap or wafer pops out. (Of course, you'll no longer have a water-saving fixture. So be sure to check local ordinances and building requirements before ditching any flow-restrictor — water-conservation requirements in your area may not allow you to remove it!)

4. If your new (or newly-fixed) shower head doesn't come with a rubber washer, wrap the threads of the pipe with a couple of go-rounds of teflon tape. Wrap clockwise (the way you'll be screwing on the shower head). Then screw on the new shower head and tighten until snug.

Unsticking the Garbage Disposal

Chicken bones, stray bottle caps, even metal screws — there's no end to the assortment of household items that seem to find their way down the sink. And such objects do NOT make a garbage disposal happy.

So you've flipped the disposal switch and nothing happened. Did *nothing* happen? Or did the garbage disposal make a faint, whining attempt? That's your first important clue.

If you can hear the disposal making an effort, there's something in there jamming the blades. If it doesn't even try, once again start with the obvious:

1. Make sure the unit is plugged in. Yes, it really does happen; sometimes moving things around under the sink can dislodge the plug, or perhaps someone unplugged the unit because the house was going to be vacant for some length of time.

2. Check the circuit breaker or fuse that serves the disposal circuit. It is possible that an overload has simply tripped the breaker or fuse.

3. If the plug is properly in place and the circuit breaker hasn't tripped, look for a reset button on the garbage disposal itself. Often the reset button is located on the bottom of the unit. Push the button and try the switch again. (On some models, the unit will automatically reset itself after 15 to 30 minutes. Let the motor cool down, and then try again.)

Still nothing? Some folks with a small hand (and a strong stomach) simply reach down inside to see if they can locate and remove the offending item. But this technique is so dangerous that frankly, I don't recommend it. (If you feel compelled to try it, be sure to turn the power off at the main breaker before beginning!)

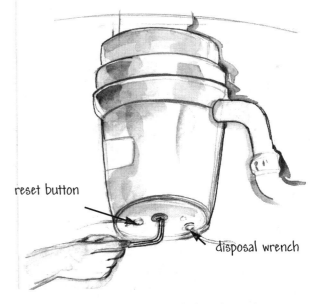

A disposal wrench can help release jams.

You may be able to remove debris with kitchen tongs or pliers. And if you're careful, persistent, and just plain lucky, you might be able to fish out a metallic object like a screw using a screwdriver with a magnetic end. (In both cases, it's still a good idea to turn the power off at the main breaker before you begin!)

If those techniques aren't able to correct the problem, there are two safer and saner methods for freeing up the disposal.

Here's what you'll need:

> **broom handle**
> **disposal wrench (one should have come with your garbage disposal) or set of allen wrenches**
> **flashlight**

4. Look underneath your garbage disposal at the very center of the unit. Some units have an indented spot to insert a disposal wrench (essentially a long allen wrench) that will allow you to turn the inside mechanism of the disposal to (hopefully) release a jam. Insert the wrench and try turning the unit. If it doesn't go in one direction, try the reverse. If you can feel the unit begin to turn freely, remove the wrench and try flipping the switch to see if the problem is solved.

5. If that doesn't work, insert the end of a broom handle down into the disposal side of the sink. Your goal here is to turn the unit so that whatever is locked up under the grinding blades is released. Push in a circular manner gently but firmly. If the unit won't turn one direction, try the reverse. CAUTION: Don't make this the next Olympic event —

if you push too hard, it's possible to loosen the entire disposal unit from its connections to the sink and drain line!

Once you feel the blades turn, remove the broom handle and try flipping the switch. Nine times out of ten, that should clear your problem. If a couple of attempts with the broom handle don't do the trick — **call in an expert** and let a professional check out the situation.

> **TIP:**
> Tape the garbage disposal wrench to the outside of the disposal unit with masking or duct tape so you can find it easily when it's needed.

⚠ CAUTIONS & CAVEATS:

- Garbage disposals are not made to operate "dry." Always turn on the faucet *before* flipping the diposal switch, and run plenty of clear, cold water while the disposal is grinding. For greasy food, follow with a healthy dose of hot water to prevent grease from clogging the drain.

- Don't be overly optimistic about the quantity of refuse your garbage disposal can handle. Feed it small quantities a little at a time, rather than expecting it to digest a huge amount at once.

- High-fiber foods may be wonderful for you, but they're not necessarily so hot for the health of your disposal. When in doubt, opt for the garbage can or compost pile.

- Never put chemical drain cleaners down your garbage disposal. Caustic chemicals can damage seals and other parts of the disposal unit.

Fixing That Drippy Faucet

Drip, drip, drip. It's torture when you're trying to fall asleep. And leaky faucets waste water, too.

Unfortunately, plumbing manufacturers seem to have taken lack of standardization to new highs (or lows) when it comes to faucet design. Every make and model is a little — and sometimes a lot — different. But here are the basics.

Faucet technology has split along two diverging lines: "compression" and "washerless" designs. Compression faucets (always two-handled, though you should remember that not all two-handled faucets are compression) use washers of one type or another to seal the unit. Washerless faucets (generally single-lever styles) use specially-designed cartridges or balls to prevent leaks.

A word of caution before you attempt any faucet repair: always turn off the water at both waterstops (those little handles under the sink); then open the faucet. If you still have a small trickle of water (or worse yet, a large trickle) coming from the spout, your waterstops are not sealing completely. You can try shutting off the water where it comes into your house, although these valves sometimes leak too. If you are unable to completely stop the trickle of water, **call in an expert** — you will need to replace the waterstops and/or main shut-off valve before proceeding.

Here are the tools & materials you'll need to get started:

screwdrivers (both flat-blade and Phillips)
crescent wrench
deep socket set
allen wrench
L-shaped seat remover
needlenose pliers
channel joint (adjustable) pliers

Compression Faucets

1. Got the water shut off? Open both faucets to drain any remaining water. Then stop up the sink and line it with paper towels or newspaper so you don't lose vital screws or washers down the drain!

   Remove the faucet handles. (Screws are generally located in the center of the knob, but may be concealed beneath the "hot" or "cold" button. Use a small screwdriver to pop off the button, if necessary. Occasionally, the handle may be held in place by an allen screw at the base.)

Pry up carefully to pop off the button.

2. A six-sided nut called a "retaining" (or "packing") nut should now be visible. Unscrew the nut (turn counter-clockwise) and then remove the stem.

Note: If the nut is set too deep to reach with a small crescent wrench, you may need to use a tube-like socket to loosen it. Inexpensive deep-socket sets are available at any hardware store. Just tell them you're working on a faucet. They'll know what you need.

> ⚠ **CAUTIONS & CAVEATS:**
> Most stems loosen counterclockwise, but a few contrarian models turn in the other direction!

3. The washer you need to replace is located on the bottom end of the stem. Turn it upside down and remove the screw holding the washer in place. SAVE THE WASHER so you can match it! Repeat the process with the other handle.

TIP:
If you have trouble loosening the screw holding the washer, temporarily put the handle back down on the stem's threads. That will give you something to hold onto to keep the stem from rotating as you turn the screwdriver.

TIP:
You really only need to replace the washer on the side that's leaking — most often the hot water side. But your tools are already out, and washers cost just pennies. Go ahead and replace both washers while you're there.

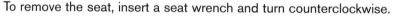

To remove the seat, insert a seat wrench and turn counterclockwise.

4. Most repair books tell you to install new replacement washers, and then test the faucets to see if they still leak — in which case you may need to replace the seats against which the washers rest as well. In my experience, by the time the washers have given up the ghost, the seats are due for replacement anyway (and often, a corroded seat is the *reason* the washer's no good).

5. The seat is a brass insert that sits down inside the hole now visible in the faucet base. Insert a seat wrench (you may need to try a couple to find the right size), and turn counterclockwise to pull out the seat.

Note: You may occasionally run into a faucet with a seat that is not removable. It IS possible to buy a seat-refinishing tool and attempt to resurface the seat. But by far your best bet for a successful outcome is to just bite the bullet and replace the entire faucet.

TIP:
"Packing" of various kinds is used to keep water from seeping up the stem around the handle. If your faucet handle leaks when the water is on (rather than the more usual drip from the spout), the problem is usually a defective O-ring, packing material or packing washer. Sometimes just tightening the packing nut a little will do the trick. Be careful not to force it, however.

6. Take the seats, washers and stems to your friendly local hardware store. Ask them to match the seats and washers exactly. In addition, if the stem contains an O-ring, packing material, or separate packing washer, get them to replace those for you as well.

7. Reassemble, turn the water back on, and check the leak. If you still hear that infamous drip, drip, drip, it's time to replace the valve stem units. Turn off the water, pull the stems, and make another trek back to the hardware store. As you'll quickly discover, many valve stems look virtually identical. Ask an experienced parts-person to help you make sure you get an exact match — and that you have both a right- and left- faucet stem in case there's a difference.

TIP:
While you've got everything apart, clean away any built-up deposits on the faucet base with a commercial lime remover.

8. Coat the threads of each new stem with a thin layer of plumber's grease or petroleum jelly to make them a little easier to remove the next time (hopefully many years from now!). Reassemble, turn the water back on, and check again.

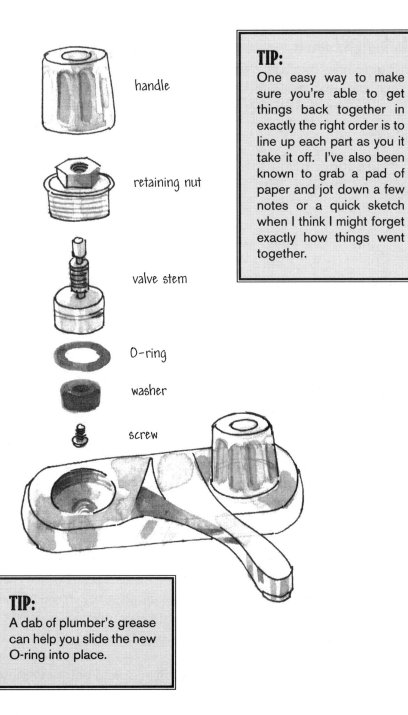

handle

retaining nut

valve stem

O-ring

washer

screw

TIP:
One easy way to make sure you're able to get things back together in exactly the right order is to line up each part as you it take it off. I've also been known to grab a pad of paper and jot down a few notes or a quick sketch when I think I might forget exactly how things went together.

TIP:
A dab of plumber's grease can help you slide the new O-ring into place.

Washerless Faucets

There are four basic types of washerless faucets: ball, cartridge, ceramic disc, and tipping valve — although of course virtually every manufacturer has its own variations on each theme.

Instructions below give a rough guide for some of the more common models. But because each manufacturer's design can be just a little different, you may need to improvise a bit.

Again, before starting to work on the faucet, be sure you TURN THE WATER OFF at both waterstops or main, turn on the faucet to empty the line, and then line the sink with paper towels or newspaper to catch any dropped parts and prevent scratches.

BALL FAUCETS

Examine the faucet handle for a setscrew (which will either be in the front or back of the handle); remove the setscrew using a small allen wrench. (Be careful not to unscrew it entirely, as it's easy to lose the little setscrew!) Using adjustable channel joint pliers with the jaws taped to protect your faucet's finish, unscrew the domed cover below by gripping it along its serrated ring.

Lift off the cam (a slotted cover in which the ball lever rides), the main seal and the ball assembly underneath. Remove the inlet seals and springs from the seat holes under the ball, using needle nose pliers or a small screwdriver. Then pull the spout assembly up and off and remove the pair of O-rings circling the outside of the faucet base.

Replace the main seal, inlet seals, springs, and pair of O-rings.

Note: A "rebuild kit" will conveniently contain all of these parts; just make certain it is expressly designed for your faucet's particular make and model.

The only real trick here comes as you reassemble the cap. You may need to play with the adjusting ring (located on the top of the domed cover) a bit to be sure that the ball lever is easy to move AND that there are no leaks around the base of the handle (turn the water back on before you put the handle back in place, just to make sure!).

CARTRIDGE FAUCETS

The water is off, right? Pop off the decorative cap on the faucet (pry up gently with a small screwdriver) and remove the handle by unscrewing the single screw underneath. You may need to raise the handle to pull it off the faucet body.

Using adjustable pliers, unscrew the retaining nut located below the handle.

The cartridge stem will now be visible. Look for a U-shaped retaining clip holding the cartridge in place inside the faucet base. (In some models the clip will be on the outside of the handle rather than underneath.)

Use a small screwdriver or needlenose pliers to carefully remove the clip.

Pull the cartridge up and out; replace with the exact same make and model. Mineral deposits can sometimes "cement" the cartridge in place. Needlenose pliers and a little patience are generally all that's required, but special cartridge-pullers are also available — ask at your hardware store. If even that doesn't work, **call in an expert;** you may need to replace the entire faucet.

While you're this far, it's a good idea to replace the O-rings around the spindle that supports the faucet body, which keep water from leaking at the base of the spout. Pull off the spout and faucet body (all one piece) and pry or cut off the old O-rings encircling the base inside. (Try to keep them relatively intact so you can buy an exact match.) Grease the two new O-rings lightly with petroleum jelly or plumber's grease and roll them into place.

Reassemble the faucet by retracing your steps. Be sure to position the new cartridge with the red "ear" facing forward (toward the sink). Test for leaks before re-attaching the handle.

You may need to work the lever to maneuver the handle back into place over the lip of the retaining nut. If hot and cold are reversed after you've replaced the cartridge, the cartridge is in "backwards"; remove the handle again and spin the cartridge 180 degrees.

CERAMIC DISC FAUCETS

Once again, make sure the water is turned off before you begin disassembling the faucet. The handle on this type of faucet may be held in place with a screw underneath the decorative cap on top, or with a set screw under the front edge of the handle, similar to those found on ball faucets.

Remove the handle and unscrew the round cap below. Remove the 2 or 3 mounting screws holding the cartridge in place and simply replace with a new matching cartridge. (In some older models, you may need to loosen the thumbscrew on the pop-up rod under the sink and remove the entire faucet body before you can reach the ceramic disc cartridge.) It IS possible to replace just the seals inside the cartridge, but for the time and effort involved you're better off buying a whole new cartridge.

TIPPING VALVE FAUCETS

Tipping valve faucets are no longer made, but you may occasionally run into one in an old-fashioned kitchen. As the name implies, these faucets have a signature "tip-able" lever mounted on a rounded cam at the back of the faucet to adjust the hot/cold water mix.

If you have inherited one of these dinosaurs, check on the availability of parts at your local hardware store before attempting repairs — it's altogether likely that parts for your model may be difficult to come by.

Occasionally fortune smiles on us, even in the midst of a plumbing project. If you're lucky enough to locate replacement parts for your unit, the repairs are fairly straightforward. (Turn the water off, of course, before you begin!) Unscrew the serrated ring at the base of the spout using channel joint (adjustable) pliers, pull off the spout, and remove the O-ring located at its base. Remove the escutcheon (housing) covering the base to reach the valves and strainers.

Unscrew the two hex-headed plugs (found one on each side of the unit), and pull out the gaskets, strainers, springs, and valve stems underneath the plugs. Using a seat wrench, remove the seats.

Clean the strainers and replace the gaskets, O-ring, and seats with new parts. Reassemble and test for leaks.

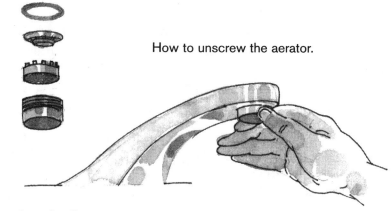

How to unscrew the aerator.

Cleaning the Aerator

I've had tenants call me in a panic over a reduced flow of water from their faucet, certain that there's something terribly wrong with the plumbing. Luckily, a gradual drop in water pressure — while disconcerting — is often simply due to a build-up of minerals and other "crud" inside the aerator on the end of the faucet nozzle.

Using your fingers or a small pair of channel joint pliers, gently turn the aerator counterclockwise.

Note: "Clockwise" and "counterclockwise" are, of course, relative terms. An aerator unscrews counterclockwise if you are looking UP at the part. Looking down at the faucet from on top, you'll appear to be turning it CLOCKWISE.

Clean out any debris you find in the screen, and screw the aerator snugly back in place.

⚠ CAUTIONS & CAVEATS:

NOT ALL aerators unscrew! Some are built right into the nozzle and simply are not made to come apart. So don't try to force matters!

Unclogging Drains

Household drains are a gravity-operated miracle — at least when they're *working* properly. When they're not, the usual culprits are hair, soap, and grease.

The good news is that many plumbing clogs occur in the trap (a U-shaped bend in the plumbing pipe that is generally pretty accessible) rather than in the main drain line itself.

Using a Plunger

Whether you've got a plugged sink or a clogged toilet, keep your fingers crossed and try the simple approach first: reach for your handy plumber's helper/plunger. Some plumbers recommend coating the rim of the plunger with a thin layer of petroleum jelly to help ensure a tight seal, but frankly I've never bothered — rubber plungers always seem to seat just fine without it, and it's just an extra mess to clean up later.

If you're dealing with a sink or tub clog, plug any overflow holes in the sink or tub with wet rags to improve the suction and make sure there are at least a couple of inches of water in the basin.

Work the plunger up and down. Start slowly, and gradually step up the pace and pressure. Give it a good two dozen plunges; rest; then try again. If the water starts to go down — mission accomplished. For really recalcitrant clogs, however, a drain snake may be necessary.

Popping Out the Lav Stopper

Sink clogs are often caused by a mucky hair/soap combination wound around the base of the lav stopper just below the drain. If plunging doesn't do the trick, it's usually a fairly simple matter to remove the stopper to see if that's what's causing the problem.

Some lav stoppers simply unscrew (use your fingers or adjustable pliers to get a good grip and turn counterclockwise). On other models, you'll need to release the stopper by unfastening the pivot rod underneath the sink that pops the stopper up and down.

Have a roll of paper towels handy. If you pull out the lav stopper and a great gob of hair and who-knows-what comes with it, pull it free with a paper towel (or three), and congratulate yourself that you've likely found the source of your problem.

Using an Auger

Sometimes the only way to effectively remove a clog is with a drain snake or auger. There are several types of augers on the market. Small, hand-cranked canister snakes often work just fine, although they do take some effort on your part to do the cranking. More professional snake models come packed into a portable drum with its own electric motor, but tend to be significantly more expensive. For toilets, the recommended tool is a "closet auger." A built-in bend in the closet auger helps angle the cable into position, while plastic-sheathed tubing protects the porcelain from scratches.

I'll assume here that you're using a typical hand-cranked canister snake. Undo the setscrew at the opening, feed out a

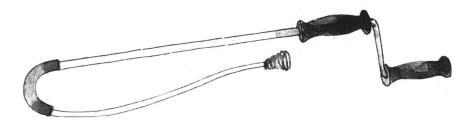

A closet auger is made for use on toilets.

short length of cable, then tighten the setscrew back down so that the cable twirls as you turn the handle. Feed the cable down the drain SLOWLY, advancing it only a few feet at a time, so that the cranking action won't kink the cable. Turn the handle as you feed to help the cable "find its way" down the twists and turns of the drainpipe.

Note: For sinks, you may need to remove the lav stopper or, better yet, disassemble and remove the trap to give you good access to the drain line.

The goal is to thread the rounded or hooked end on the cable down to the clog, so that you'll be able to snag the offending material, or break it up to allow it to flush properly on down the drain line. This procedure takes PATIENCE and a certain amount of luck; you may need to try and then try again. I've been elated to find items like a plastic thread spool or a cotton swab suddenly show up skewered on the end of the snake after 15 minutes to an hour of trying.

If you don't seem to be able to thread the auger successfully down through the fixture or if your auger doesn't seem to be long enough to reach the clog, check around for a clean-out plug that may allow you easier access to the main plumbing run serving the fixture.

Clean-out plugs look like round caps, with a raised square-sided "nut" on the top for easy gripping with a crescent or pipe wrench. Sometimes there will be a small clean-out plug at the bend in a trap itself. Clean-outs may also be located along baseboards (especially in rather inconspicuous locations like garages and closets), or along the foundation outside your house.

If you locate a clean-out, unscrew the cover (turn counter-clockwise with a crescent or pipe wrench). Because they're not used often, clean-out caps can be tough to open. If necessary, tap gently on your wrench with a hammer in the direction you're trying to turn, to help loosen the threads. (However much you might feel like releasing your frustrations, however, skip the brute force — especially with plastic lids and pipe.)

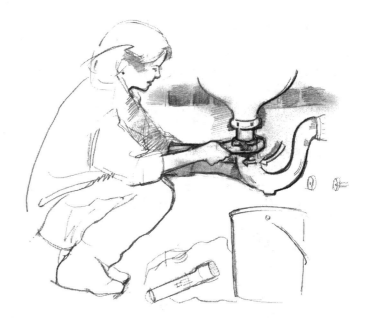

Tightening the trap fittings.

the clog with your hand-held auger. For tougher clogs (those caused by invasive tree roots, for example), you may need to call in a professional drain service, which will have bigger, meaner cutting-tipped snakes.

Opening Traps
Here are the tools & materials you'll need to get started:

> **CAUTIONS & CAVEATS:**
> Always open a clean-out s-l-o-w-l-y – depending on where the clog is, there could be LOTS of water trapped there, ready to spew out! If water begins seeping around the threads as you loosen the clean-out plug, it may be a good idea to wait a few hours to give the water time to go down. (Most clogs don't completely close the line.) If you still find water beginning to seep out later as you crack it open, either be prepared for a terrific mess – **or call in an expert!**

pipe wrench
bucket or bowl to catch leaks
penetrating oil (for metal pipes only)
flashlight

Once the clean-out is open, feed the cable in slowly, cranking as you go. You will usually feel resistance when it reaches the clog. With any luck, you'll be able to dislodge or remove

Most tubs and sinks have (or SHOULD have) an easily-accessible trap underneath the fixture. (Toilets generally have the trap-bend molded into the porcelain fixture itself.)

If judicious plunging doesn't seem to solve your problem, opening the trap may help you more easily reach the clog.

Look for the flat-sided couplings near the ends of the "U" of the trap (these, like the trap itself, may be made of either metal or plastic). Place a bucket underneath to catch any leaks or drips.

Using a pipe wrench, turn the coupling nut counterclockwise. (It's not always easy at first to figure out which way IS counterclockwise... If it doesn't go one way, try the other!) BE AS GENTLE AS YOU CAN. You don't want to break the plastic or damage old and possibly fragile metal pipe. If necessary, apply penetrating oil — and wait! (Useful for metal pipes only, of course.)

Once you loosen the couplings, push the fittings up out of the way, pull out the U-shaped trap section, and take a close look inside the trap with your flashlight. If there's evidence of a clog, use a wire coat hanger to gently work it free.

While you've got it off, also check the condition of the trap and drainpipe material itself. All too often (especially with metal pipe) you'll discover that the trap is corroded, damaged, and just waiting to spring a leak.

If you replace the trap with a plastic section, be forewarned: plastic has an uncanny way of loosening itself up. Check it frequently over the next few days and weeks to make sure the trap hasn't developed a small leak. The couplings may need to be tightened up a tad.

Using Chemical Drain Cleaners

You'll run into all sorts of conflicting advice when it comes to chemical drain cleaners. Some folks recommend using them regularly to keep all drains in your house running free. Others recommend that you NEVER use chemical cleaners, claiming that the caustic chemicals may not be good for your plumbing or that if they don't do the trick, they'll only make your subsequent efforts with a plunger or auger more dangerous and difficult.

Chemical drain cleaners DO seem to work best on slow (but not completely clogged) sink drains where the culprit is a build-up of hair, soap and/or grease. They are generally not recommended for completely clogged drains or for toilet clogs.

If you do decide to try a chemical drain opener, be sure to read package instructions CAREFULLY before you begin. Wear protective goggles and heavy rubber gloves. If your house is on a septic system, make sure you buy a product that is rated as safe for septic systems.

Other Possible Clog Problems

Dishwashers and garbage disposals are prone to food-related clogs. Most dishwashers have a little plastic strainer at the bottom which can be lifted out for easy cleaning. For a stopped-up garbage disposal, see the section Unsticking the Garbage Disposal above.

> **TIP:**
> To prevent future clogs, install filters or screens on all sinks and shower drains to catch excess hair, bits of soap, etc.

If All Else Fails. . .

Professional drain-cleaning services have high-powered equipment, long snakes, and lots of experience with all sorts of plumbing clogs. Sometimes they'll be able to access a particularly difficult clog by climbing up on your roof and running their snake down through the vent line — often a straighter shot to the main drain line than can be reached by working from inside the house.

Retrieving Wedding Rings, Etc.

It's all too easy to drop a piece of jewelry down the bathroom sink. But Aunt Sophie's solid gold heirloom hatpin or your diamond-encrusted earring may not be lost forever. Particularly with heavier objects, their very weight may save the day — causing them to settle in the trap underneath the sink.

You'll want to IMMEDIATELY turn off any water that may be running in the sink to keep from flushing the object any further down the line. Grab a bucket and your trusty pipe wrench, and, following the instructions above, open the sink's trap.

Carefully tip the trap upside down into the bucket — with a bit of luck, that "ker-plunk!" you hear is the happy ending to the story!

Recaulking a Tub

Is the old caulk around your tub pulling away from the wall or discolored from mildew? Caulking repairs are simple and can quickly improve the look of a bathroom.

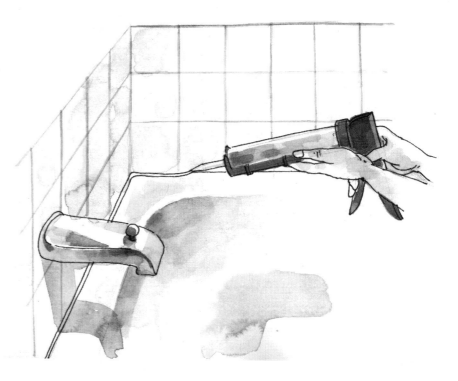

The sheer variety of caulking compounds now available can be rather bewildering. The primary distinctions include whether the product is intended for interior or exterior use; whether it can be used in high-moisture areas; what materials it is made to adhere to (some don't bond well to metals or masonry); whether it's paintable; and whether it requires solvent or just water for clean-up. Read the labels carefully to make sure you're getting a caulk that's formulated for the application you have in mind.

For bathroom use, look for a caulking material that is designed for high-moisture areas and is mildew-resistant. If you'll be caulking against a painted wall, make sure the caulk is also paintable in case you need to do any touch-ups. (But don't buy plain painter's caulk by mistake. It's not made to be

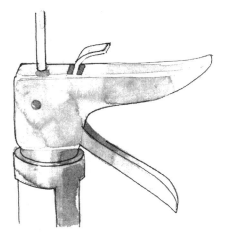

The release latch allows you to retract the plunger.

used in wet or damp conditions.)   New, pretinted caulks now come in a variety of designer colors for bathrooms with colored fixtures.

Here's what you'll need:

> **small putty knife**
> **razor knife**
> **caulk**
> **caulking gun**
> **16-penny nail or piece of heavy wire**
> **paper towels**
> **bucket of water**
> **caulk finishing tool (optional)**

1. Remove as much of the old caulk as possible, using the small putty knife to gently scrape it away from the tub and wall. Be careful not to scratch or gouge. Sometimes you can remove the last little bits with a mildly abrasive cleaning pad or fiber-backed sponge (what we call a "green scrubbie" around our house).

2. Make sure the area you'll be caulking is free of grit and perfectly dry. Insert the tube of caulk into your caulking gun (pull back on the L-shaped lever at the back end. Sometimes there is a release latch you have to push near the trigger or on the back of the handle to get the plunger to retract.) The only trick to remember in using a caulking gun is that "off" is when the tail of the L-shaped lever is pointing down, and "on" is when the tail points up. For now, keep the lever angled down/off.

3. With your razor knife, cut open the end of the spout by making a small cut toward the very end (rest the end of the spout against a piece of scrap lumber and cut AWAY from yourself). There are two schools of thought on caulking technique here. Some painting professionals prefer a caulking spout with a diagonal cut, while others swear a perfectly straight cut leaves a better bead. Personally, I'm a diagonal-cut fan, but you can experiment with both and decide which works best for you.

   Remember that caulk comes out fast, so keep the opening smaller than you want the caulk joint to be. The tube has a seal inside the spout that must be punctured to start the flow of caulk. Push a 16-penny nail or stout piece of wire firmly down the spout opening to break the seal.

4. Turn the L-shaped rod so the tail points up, and squeeze the handle a few times to "queue up" the caulk in the gun. You may want to practice starting and stopping the flow of caulk over an old piece of newspaper just to get a feel for it. Once

> **TIP:**
> A possible alternative for the caulking-gun-impaired: At least one manufacturer now offers caulk in a pressurized can – just invert the can and press the nozzle.

you feel comfortable, push the point of the tube into the crevice to be caulked, gently squeeze the trigger, and move the gun slowly and steadily along. If you're right-handed, start at the leftmost corner and work toward your right. If you're left-handed, start at the rightmost corner.

5. If you're really, REALLY good, you can get a professional-looking bead right from the caulking gun. For the rest of us, it takes a little work to "finish" the bead. Any painting or hardware store can sell you a little plastic caulk finishing tool that half-pushes, half-scrapes the caulk into a nice, clean line. If you decide to just use the "wet-finger" technique, dampen your finger in a bucket of water and *gently* glide it along the seam. Be sure not to use too much water or you may dilute the caulk and keep it from creating a tight seal. Scrape up any excess with a damp paper towel and/or a light swipe with your putty knife.

6. That's it! Just be sure to let the caulk dry thoroughly (read package instructions for exact curing time) before you use the tub.

Installing Lawn Sprinklers

If you've ever crisped an expensive shrub because you completely forgot about it while you went off on vacation or chafed at having to hand-water the lawn every evening, you'll appreciate the convenience of automatic sprinklers.

Installing plastic sprinkler pipe is sort of a cross between an arts-and-crafts session and playing with a kid's erector set. Just line everything up, swab the parts with glue, fit them together, and *voila!*

The only difficult part about adding a sprinkler system is tapping into the water main somewhere near where the line enters your house. If you're not thoroughly confident with your plumbing skills, I'd suggest you hire an expert for that little job. Just explain that you'll need a water supply line for sprinklers, and make sure that your plumber includes a separate shut-off valve for the new sprinkler line. Keep this new line capped until you're ready to start installing the sprinklers.

"Automatic" sprinklers mean, of course, that power will be necessary to run them. So plan ahead for the location of your timer. You'll need to run a small (Number 18) wire from the sprinkler valve(s) to the spot where you plan to mount your timer inside the house. The timer will also have a transformer unit that will need to be plugged into a grounded house

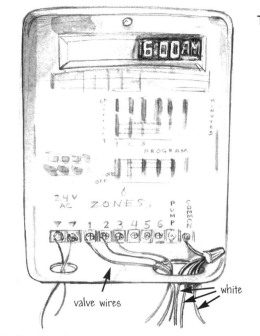

The timer box

valve wires

white

power in from transformer

outlet. If possible, try to pick a location for the timer that's both convenient to an inside outlet and not very far away from your new sprinkler water supply line.

Most of the major sprinkler supply manufacturers now offer free "computerized design" services by mail. You'll need to provide them with a to-scale drawing of your property, with house, landscaping, and water meter location marked. You'll also need to tell them the size of your water meter (usually stamped right on the side of the meter); the diameter of your water supply line (if in doubt, wrap a string around the pipe leading from your water meter to the house — the sprinkler manufacturer can help you convert that circumference information to a diameter reading); the distance from the meter to your house; and your static water pressure (borrow or purchase a pressure gauge, and take readings at your outside faucets). Some manufacturers now sell computer software that will allow you to design your own sprinkler set-up.

It's also a good idea to check with your local building department and water company about any codes or requirements that may apply to sprinkler systems in your area. Some city codes require antisiphon-style valves, for example, to prevent backflow into the city's water system.

Shoot off all of that information by mail and within a couple of weeks you should receive a complete parts list and sprinkler system design custom-tailored for your home, plus a "how-to" installation guide. (The manufacturer is being so helpful, of course, because they want you to buy THEIR brand!)

You'll most likely end up with a stack of ten-foot lengths of white Schedule 40 PVC (polyvinyl chloride) pipe, a small bucketfull of connectors, adaptors, elbows, risers and sprinkler heads, one or more automatic valves, and a 2-, 4- or 6-station timer. Now comes the fun part.

In addition to your list of parts, here's what you'll need:

PVC glue
hacksaw or plastic pipe cutter
trenching shovel
stakes
hammer

Working with PVC (polyvinyl chloride)

Working with PVC is just about as simple as cut and paste. Cut the pipe to length using a hacksaw or plastic pipe cutter. To join sections of pipe with a connector or to add fittings, swab both the inside of the part and the end of the pipe to be joined with PVC cement. Push the parts firmly together and twist gently back and forth for just a second to make sure the glue is making a good contact.

PVC cement sets up in a hurry. Give it a minute or two to dry completely before adding the next section.

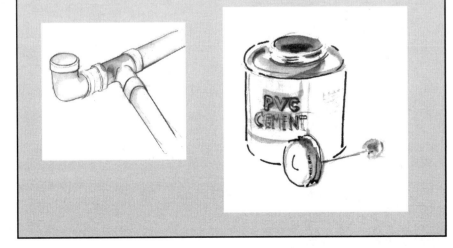

1. Drive a stake or marker at each location on your layout where you plan to have a sprinkler head.

2. Dig a shallow (6- to 8-inch) trench between the sprinkler heads along the lines called out on your design plan. Sprinkler line doesn't have to be buried very deep; if you live in an area subject to freezing, however, you should shut off and drain the system before the first frost to prevent damage to the system.

Dig a shallow trench according to your design plan.

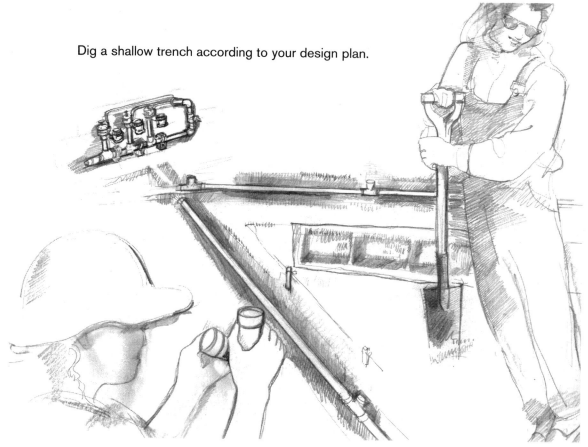

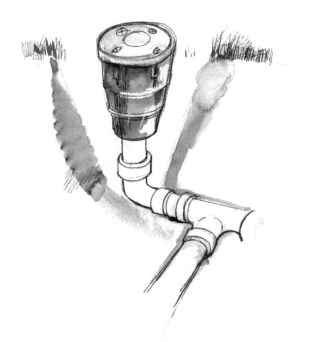

An attached sprinkler head.

3. Follow the manufacturer's recommendations for installing the sprinkler valve or valves on your new sprinkler line. Typically, this involves constructing a "manifold" that will provide water to two or more valves. Make sure the risers hold the valves at least 6-8 inches above ground, and space the valves about 8 inches away from each other.

4. "Follow the dots" and connect the pipe as called for on your plan from the sprinkler valves to the location of each sprinkler head. If you live in a cold-weather area, make

Automatic sprinkler valves are put together to form a manifold.

sure the designer has included a way to drain your system completely before winter sets in. (If they've forgotten to do this, just make sure you have a removable screw-plug or self-draining valve at the lowest point on your system.)

5. Test each circuit in the system by manually opening the valves, one at a time, to make sure there are no leaks before you bury the pipe.

Hooking Up the Wiring to the Valves

For your sprinklers to operate automatically, you'll need to run wires from the timer to each of your newly-installed valves.

Each valve is controlled by a pair of tiny wires — a hot and a neutral. Measure carefully and buy a length of sprinkler-control wire (generally, a sheathed cable containing several Number 18 wires inside it) long enough to run from your timer box out to the location of your valve assembly. To determine the number of wires you'll need to have inside the cable, count up the number of valves you've installed and add one extra for the white (neutral) wire.

Run the cable from the spot where you plan to install your timer through the basement, or in other out-of-the-way locations, to a point opposite the valve location. Drill a small (3/8 or 1/2 inch) hole through the outside wall near the valves, being careful not to drill into existing electrical or plumbing runs! Feed the cable through a plastic drinking straw, if necessary, to help "fish" it through the wall.

Hook up a different colored wire to one of the two leads on each sprinkler valve. Join the white (neutral) wire to the other lead on each sprinkler valve.

At the timer box, read the manufacturer's instructions to determine the proper screw terminal for the white (neutral) wire. Connect the colored wires one by one to terminal screws designated by the manufacturer for individual circuits.

Connect the leads from the transformer wire (do NOT plug the transformer in yet!) to their own designated terminal screws. Plug in the transformer and test it to make sure the individual circuits work properly. Then seal around the wires where they penetrate the wall with a dab of weatherproof caulk.

Chapter 3

MECHANICAL and DECORATIVE PROJECTS

Changing Locks & Deadbolts

The world's worst roommate finally moved out — and you want to make sure she doesn't decide to move back in. Your nosy neighbor has a habit of showing up for coffee unannounced. Or perhaps you just want a sleek new look for your doors.

There are lots of reasons why you might want to change your locks. And if you've ever priced a locksmith's services, you've got that much more incentive to learn the basics yourself.

Choosing the Right Parts

Be sure you buy the right type of doorset for the application you have in mind. Typically, your hardware store will offer these choices:

- keyed entry set (generally used on outside doors; may come packaged with or without a deadbolt)

- bed/bath or "privacy" set (with a button-lock on one side)
- hall/closet or "passage" set (non-locking)
- dummy knob (knob only, without a latch)

You *can* buy deadbolts separately, but for convenience's sake you're usually better off to purchase a "keyed-alike" combination package that includes a doorset and deadbolt that open with the same key. Similarly, if you're doing a front and back door at the same time, look for pre-packaged sets that use the same key for all locks.

As with most other things in life, when it comes to door locks you get what you pay for. But you don't necessarily need to purchase the top-of-the-line product to get a high-quality, durable lock. Even relatively inexpensive brands will give you years of flawless service.

Take a close look, however, before buying the cheapest model on the shelf. As a cost-cutting measure, some manufacturers are now using plastic for the latch and other interior

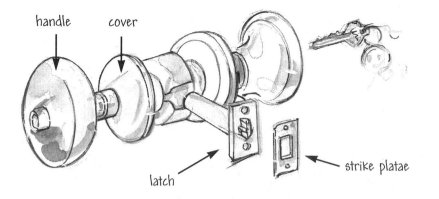

handle   cover

latch

strike platae

parts on their low-end doorsets. The trade-off, of course, is durability. Pass on the plastic and spend a couple of extra bucks for a model with all-metal parts.

Deadbolts come in two varieties: those that require a key to open the lock from both sides, and those that take a key from the outside but can be opened with a knob on the inside. The double-keyed variety provides the best security, especially if the door is located near a window or contains a pet door; even if burglars break the glass or reach through the pet door, they won't be able to undo the lock. But double-keyed deadbolts can also pose a dangerous obstacle in case of fire, unless you keep a key in the deadbolt whenever you're home. Which type of deadbolt is best is a judgment call you'll have to make based on your own situation and preferences.

How They Work

We take doorsets for granted, but they're actually rather ingenious mechanical devices. Just exactly how they are constructed is different from brand to brand and model to model. But all operate in basically the same way.

A turn of the handle is converted into a side-to-side force that retracts the latch, allowing the door to open. In the case of a locking doorset, the unit also contains a device that can "put the brakes on" this turning movement and prevent the door from being opened.

If you want your new lock set to take the same key as an existing door lock, you'll probably need to call a locksmith. You can save a little money by taking the locks off and bringing them with you to the locksmith, rather than paying for a service call. (Be sure to have someone stay at home while the locks are gone, of course, for security reasons!) If the old and new locks are different makes, call ahead — not all brands will accept the same key blank. One do-it-yourself alternative: buy two new locks that are already keyed alike and replace both locks!

Whether you're changing a front door lock or just a hall closet doorset, don't let the complex-looking mechanism scare you. Grab your screwdriver and jump in!

Here are the tools & materials you'll need to get started:

* **Phillips screwdriver**
* **small flat-blade screwdriver (for certain models)**
* **new lock or doorset**
* **knife (to cut open packaging)**

1. Locate the two screws at the base of one of the *handles* (not the ones on the edge of the door holding the latch). The screws are usually on the "inside" or locking side of the door.

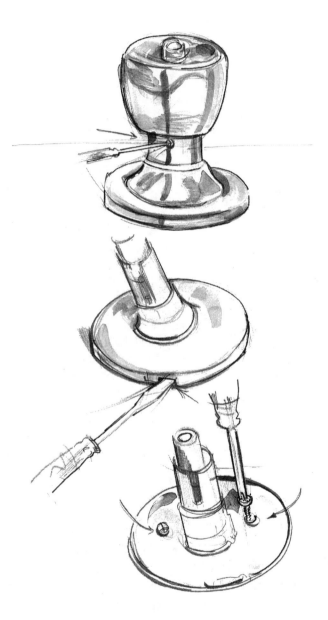

You may need to remove the handle and a metal cover to access the screws underneath.

Note: While the screws are plainly visible in most models, a few manufacturers conceal the screws beneath a metal cover. For these, you'll need a tiny screwdriver or a pointed knife to remove the handle and metal cover. Look for a slot at the base of the handle about a half inch long with a tab showing through. Push in on the tab to release the handle, a similar technique to changing the attachments on a vacuum. Then look for a small, square opening around the edge of the cover. Insert the blade and pry up gently to pop off the cover.

2. Use your Phillips-head screwdriver to remove the two screws that hold the lock together, and gently pull the two handles apart. (The base touching the door may stick a bit if the door has been painted. You may also need to press in the latch to release the spring tension against the barrel.)

3. Locate the two screws holding the latch (on the narrow edge of the door). Unscrew and gently remove the latch.

4. Open the package containing your new doorset and install the new latch section first. Make sure the angled edge of the tongue is facing TOWARD the doorframe so that it will slip into position properly.

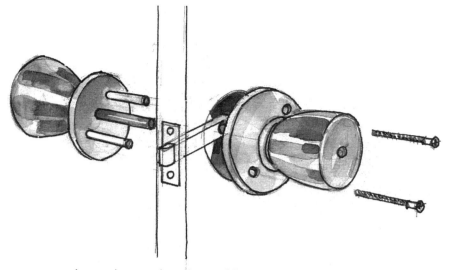

Insert the new handles and line up the screws

5. Insert the handles, one from each side, and secure with the new long screws that came with the package. This part is a bit touchier than they make it look in package directions. It can take a little wiggling and jiggling to get each screw properly aligned with the hole on the other side. Push in on the knob on the opposite side of the door from you, so that it sits flush against the door; leave your side a bit loose until you get one screw started. Don't tighten more than a few turns before starting the second screw.

6. Tighten both screws until they are snug; the handles should be firm against the door and should operate easily. If the latch mechanism binds, re-loosen both screws and adjust the fit; then tighten again.

Note: This discussion assumes your existing door hardware is of the modern *cylindrical* or *tubular* type found in most homes built from about the 1950s on. Older homes may have what

TIPS:
- Doors that have been forced (especially common in households where one spouse has a propensity for locking him- or herself in the bathroom) may exhibit what I call "loose latch syndrome" — the short screws that are supposed to hold the latch in place will no longer tighten down into the wood. One simple fix is to purchase longer screws. You can also insert a piece of a wooden match or a small sliver of wood into the over-enlarged screw hole to take up room and give the screw something to tighten against. (Add a dab of carpenter's glue before inserting the bit of wood to help hold it in place.) If those halfway measures don't solve the problem, however, the "real" fix is to replace the entire door — a project best left for an expert!

- Don't throw away those little crook-necked pins that come in the package with your new door lock. Each pin is essentially a "skeleton key" that will allow you to open a locked bathroom or bedroom door from the outside — especially handy for families with young kids! Just insert the straight end of the pin into the hole in the outside of the door, and twist. Practice once or twice before you put it away so you'll see how it works. Then keep a pin or two in a convenient drawer, just in case.

are known as *mortise locks*: elongated metal-cased units that are "mortised" (cut and recessed) into the door. If the metal latch plate on your door's edge is tall and skinny (that is, more than about 2 inches long), you probably have a mortise lock. It IS possible to replace old mortise locks with a newer type of door hardware, but it requires plugging the old mortised cut and re-drilling the door. Commercial "conversion kits" are available, but unless you're totally comfortable with a hole saw and chisel, it's a job best left for someone with experience.

Hanging a Heavy Picture or Mirror

The best way to support a heavy picture or mirror is by driving a nail or other fastener directly into a stud. But finding a stud by the "knock, knock" method is always easier said than done.

Invest in a battery-operated studfinder and learn to use it. It'll save you hours of trouble spackling and repainting all those "it's gotta be here somewhere" test holes.

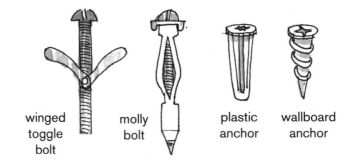

winged toggle bolt   molly bolt   plastic anchor   wallboard anchor

Lighter-Duty Hanging Jobs

For lighter-duty applications where finding a stud is not as critical, there are a variety of good fasteners on the market.

Move the studfinder from side to side; the lights will tell you when you're over a stud.

TIP:
• Studs are generally located 16 inches apart, center-to-center. So if you find one stud that's not quite where you need it, chances are there's another 16 inches away on either side.
• Avoid driving nails in any area likely to contain plumbing or electrical runs. This includes walls with plumbing fixtures on the other side, or any section of wall above a light fixture, switch or outlet.

TIP:
Know before You Go: To select the correct fastener, a salesperson will likely ask you the type of surface (drywall; plaster; masonry) you're trying to fasten into; and for drywall, they'll ask about the thickness. Most drywall is either 1/2 inch or 5/8 inch. To determine the dimension of your particular wall, carefully drill a small hole in the area where you plan to use the fastener. (This is one case where you want to use a studfinder to make sure you *won't* be hitting a stud!) Insert a small nail, head side first, into the hole, and angle it slightly so the head catches on the back side of the drywall. Grip the shank of the nail with your fingers at the wall's edge, then withdraw the nail and measure the distance between your fingers and the nailhead.

TIP:
If at First You Don't Succeed: Don't try to resurrect a failed mounting effort. If the fasteners holding a towel bar pull out, for example, don't simply replace them with bigger anchors — start fresh. Move the entire towel bar over several inches on the wall, secure with new, heavy-duty fasteners and patch the old holes.

Screw-in, self-drilling metal anchors, for example, are excellent for mounting lightweight items such as small pictures or kitchen accessories on drywall. For moderate loads, a Molly bolt (hollow wall anchor) or a metal or plastic toggle will provide more secure mounting. When in doubt, ask your friendly hardware store salesperson to help you choose a fastener for the application you have in mind.

Painting

There's nothing that transforms a room — or a house — like a coat of paint. It's wonderful to watch grimy walls (and someone else's color scheme) disappear under a blanket of basic white. Even that pungent new-paint smell screams fresh and clean.

The trick to a good paint job is, of course, good preparation. Let's take a look at the basics:

Prepping a Room
Here are the tools & materials you'll need to get started:

whisk broom & dustpan
rags
screwdriver (flat-blade)
coffee can or small bucket
claw hammer   **masking tape**
spackle   **masker**
putty knife   **rolls of masking paper**
stepladder   **dropcloths**
primer-sealer   **(preferably heavy canvas)**

masking tape

putty knife

DROPCLOTH

Note: The discussion here assumes you have determined that lead paint is NOT present in your home. If lead paint is present, special precautions will be necessary. Contact the National Lead Clearinghouse (NLC) at 1-800-424-LEAD for detailed advice.

- Ideally, the room you're planning to paint will be empty. If that's not possible, remove as many smaller objects as possible to other parts of the house and take down curtains or other window treatments. Enlist some helpers to shove any remaining furniture to the center of the room, where it can be protected with dropcloths. Try to give yourself as much clear working space as possible around the room's perimeter. You can imagine the sorts of disasters that can involve slipping, tripping, and buckets of wet paint.

- Remove pictures, bulletin boards, nails, and thumbtacks. Unless you're positive you want to hang an item back in the exact same spot, spackle the holes. Patch any cracks or holes in the wall while you're at it.

> **TIP:**
> Open fine cracks with a putty knife or old-fashioned "churchkey"-type can opener to give spackle a firmer grip.

- Take a close look at trim and molding. Has it already been painted over so many times it's losing its definition? If it's really unsightly, you might consider stripping off the old layers with a chemical stripper (look for one that does not contain methylene chloride, if possible) or use a heat gun. On the other hand, this is a big job. Decide if it's really worth your time and effort.

- Wash down any exceptionally dirty walls. Treat any spots that might bleed through (water marks; grease; lipstick; ink; crayon) with a spritz of pigmented primer-sealer. Run your whisk broom over window ledges and around baseboards; then follow with a damp rag.

- Using your screwdriver, remove switchplate and outlet covers. (I throw all the screws and covers in a small bucket for safekeeping.) It's always a good idea turn the power off first, just as a precaution. I'll admit — I don't usually bother when I'm just removing covers. But there ARE live wires in those boxes.

- Mask off windows, doorknobs, light switches, outlets, and phone jacks. Also mask any wood-finish trim or paneling adjoining a painted area. If you plan on replacing the carpeting anyway, don't worry about masking at the baseboard. Otherwise, to protect the existing carpeting or hardwood floors, run a strip of masking paper around the

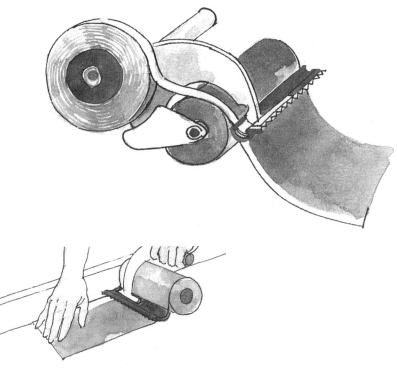

Using a masker can speed up prep work.

⚠️ **CAUTIONS & CAVEATS:**

Sanding, scraping and heating lead paint can pose a serious health threat, particularly to children and pregnant women. If your home was built before 1978, there is a good possibility that some or all of the older coats of paint on your walls and woodwork contain lead. Special precautions need to be taken in order to safely work with lead paint. Contact the National Lead Clearinghouse (NLC) for advice (1-800-424-LEAD).

Home test kits (especially those which provide mail-in laboratory results) claim to be able to detect lead in paint and other materials with a high degree of accuracy (See Chapter 5). Do-it-yourself indicator tests, though obviously less accurate than sophisticated laboratory analysis, can also be useful and may help flag the need for further testing.

You may also want to consider **calling in an expert.** The NLC maintains a centralized listing of individuals and organizations who provide services such as lead-based paint inspections, risk assessments, and hazard control services. Call 1-888-LEADLIST for information.

---

perimeter of the room (tape it a few inches up along the baseboard — you'll be cutting in the edges anyway). Then lay dropcloths on the floor overlapping the edge of the masking paper.

- *Don't* wrap overhead light fixtures with masking paper if you're going to need them on for light. Better yet, bring in a freestanding light you don't mind getting paint-speckled.

Calculating Coverage

Okay, the room's all ready and you've chosen the color and type of paint you want to buy. How MUCH paint will you need?

For a precise figure, bring the room's dimensions with you to the paint store and get them to help you calculate exactly how many gallons to buy, based on the coverage-per-gallon estimate provided by the manufacturer. As a general rule of thumb, expect to use about 1-1/2 gallons of flat to paint an average-sized bedroom (including ceiling), and a little under one gallon of semi-gloss for a normal bathroom. (If you're painting over a darker color, of course, it may take more than one coat to cover.)

TIP:
Trying to match the "orangepeel" or "knockdown" coat of textured drywall used to be nearly impossible without professional help. But repairs now can be blended easily and virtually undetectably, thanks to touch-up kits that come in a spray can. Ask at your local hardware store.

Buy a whole gallon of trim paint, even if you figure that a quart would do. A gallon is cheap enough and it's always good to have a little extra on hand for touch-ups.

The Great Primer Debate

Should you bother with a primer coat? That depends on what you're painting over. *Always* use a primer if you're painting bare wood. Primer is also recommended on sooty or chalky surfaces, as a first coat on new drywall, or to improve adhesion if you're planning to use latex over a surface previously painted with an oil-based paint. Because primer tends to be less expensive than regular paint, you might also consider using a primer coat when you know two or more coats will be needed to cover over a darker color.

Whenever you use primer, ask your paint store to tint the primer close to (but a bit lighter than) the shade you'll be using for the final color coat to improve coverage. (If both primer and finish coat are exactly the same color, it's hard to tell if you missed a spot!)

Additives

Professional painters have a couple of great tricks up their sleeve that you should know about. If you're facing deteriorated, slick or chalky surfaces, or if mildew has been a problem, ask a knowledgeable clerk at your painting supply or hardware store about the following additives:

Bonding Agents: Stir-in bonding agents can help improve the adhesion of latex paint to chalky or dusty walls, or to metal surfaces such as aluminum siding.

Mildecides: If mildew is a problem in your area, consider adding a mildecide to each gallon of paint. (Remember, however, that mildecide is only a deterrent; it can't cure an underlying problem caused by inadequate ventilation, moisture seep, and so on.) Be sure to clean mildewed surfaces THOROUGHLY with a diluted bleach/detergent solution and allow to dry before repainting.

Painting Tips & Techniques

Itching to crack that can of paint?

Here are the tools & materials you'll need to get started:

> **screwdriver or paint can opener, or (for 5-gallon buckets) razor knife**
> **stir stick**
> **empty 5-gallon bucket**
> **bucket screen**
> **paint strainer or old pair of nylons**
> **paint roller & extension handle**
> **roller cover**
> **angled sash brush**
> **goggles**

Just a word about selecting painting equipment before we get going. You'll find that roller covers come in various nap depths. For a smooth surface, a thin-napped roller works best, while a thick, heavy pile helps get the paint into the cracks and crevices of stucco or other heavily-textured surfaces. Unless you're painting the inside of a garage or similar area where finish really doesn't matter, skip the "economy" roller covers, which tend to shed and don't hold paint well.

Cheap roller frames are more trouble than they're worth. I had one frustrating painting day where I broke two in a row and had to stop everything and dash to the store to buy a third. Especially when you're using a roller handle extension, there's a lot of stress and strain on the roller's handle. Buy the extra-sturdy edition with a metal-reinforced handle. (Better yet, buy two just in case!)

Myself, I use a 2-inch angled polyester-bristle brush for just about every paint job. It carries a reasonable amount of paint without getting unbearably heavy, and the angle helps to get a clean line even in tight places. But it's really a matter of personal preference. Some folks prefer

> **TIP:**
> Don't try to use natural (China bristle) brushes for any paint that calls for water clean-up. The water soaks into the bristles and it's like trying to paint with wet noodles. (Read the label clean-up instructions, even for "oil-based" products. We recently discovered our mistake too late when trying to brush on a specially-formulated "oil" deck stain.)

a straight-cut brush, and for really tricky spots like cutting in around window panes, a smaller brush may give you better control. Try a variety of sizes and styles of paintbrush and see which YOU prefer.

Ready to roll? Let's go!

roller handle extension

roller

roller cover

paint can opener

angled sash brush

mildecide

5-gallon bucket and screen

paint tray

Choosing Paint

Before you get carried away trying to choose the perfect color among all those little color chips at the paint store, you've got one BASIC decision to make: latex or oil-based paint?

Latex, of course, is the hands-down winner for easy clean-up. Just rinse rollers and brushes in water, and they're ready for the next project. Latex paint is also faster-drying than oil-based paints, and less smelly in the process. Add the fact that it tends to be somewhat cheaper, and it's little wonder that latex paint has become so popular.

Oil-based paint has changed a lot in recent years to keep up with air quality and health requirements. Gone are the days when lead was a key ingredient and nobody cared about volatile organic compounds (VOCs). Today's "oil-based" paint is actually alkyd, a lead-free blend of oil and synthetic resin formulated to minimize emissions.

Even with these changes, oil-based paint still makes up in durability what it lacks in easy clean-up. For high-traffic areas where you need a long-lasting, scrubable finish, oil-based paint is still the way to go.

One other important consideration before you pick a side in the great latex/oil dilemma: what type of paint will you be painting *over*? While oil paint works fine on walls formerly painted with latex, you can run into problems if you try to use latex paint to cover a previously oil-painted wall. (Picture a saggy, droopy mess that's adhered just well enough to make it a real chore to scrape back off!) While you *can* primer an oil-painted wall to allow painting over with latex, this is an extra step you may prefer to avoid.

If you're not sure what kind of paint is presently on your walls, at least one manufacturer now makes a home test kit that lets you check to see whether it's latex or oil.

Once you've crossed that all-important latex-or-oil hurdle, go ahead — immerse yourself in a sea of color charts and chips. Just remember that light colors tend to make a room look bigger, darker shades make the area look smaller, and any color will have a tendency to look much

more *intense* when you get a whole roomful of it. Unless you're really going for shock value, err on the side of more neutral tones and choose gentle shade variations rather than sharply contrasting colors.

Paints come in a variety of finishes (flat, eggshell, satin, semi-gloss, gloss). As a general rule, use flat paint for bedrooms and living areas, and semi-gloss for doors, trim, bathrooms and kitchens. Some folks like to use the easier-to-wash semi-gloss for children's rooms as well. If you're tempted to go one step up to a gloss finish, just remember that shiny surfaces are less forgiving. Every little dimple and flaw in the wall's surface will stand out that much more under glossier paint.

And as for quality (one more time!): you get what you pay for. Your local paint store can probably mix up that same shade of dusty rose using a low-, medium- or high-grade paint base. The major difference in paints is the amount of pigment — which will affect, among other things, how well it covers. You could wind up using two coats of the super-cheapo brand where one of the premium paint would do. Go for at least a medium grade. And if you don't plan to move for a while, spring for the big bucks and do it up right. Good paint pays for itself in the long run.

If you're buying a pre-tinted color, have the clerk put the can or bucket into their paint shaking machine to save yourself some time and trouble stirring it up later. If the store does a custom-mix for you, they'll automatically mix it. But be sure they open the can and CHECK the color by daubing it against your paint swatch before you leave the store. If you think mistakes never happen, let me tell you about our little experience painting a rental house a glorious pumpkin-color....

> **TIP:**
> Protect the coded mixing label that your paint store affixes to the can by covering it with a wide piece of clear plastic box tape — that's crucial information that can help you match the paint exactly at a later date, if necessary. Just as a back-up, I also jot the mixing code down on the original color chip and stash it in a file folder for future reference.

1. Pop open your paint can, stir thoroughly, and dump it into the empty 5-gallon bucket (preferably over a piece of newspaper, just in case). If you've got more than one can (and especially if some of the paint is old and some new), it's a good idea to mix the paint together to ensure a uniform color. Be sure to stir the mixture well. A paint tray is another option, but to me it's just one more thing to clean up.

   If you're using old paint that's been sitting around, strain the paint through a paint filter or pair of old nylons to remove any crud that may have built up in the can before adding to your fresh, clean bucket.

   DON'T fill your 5-gallon bucket completely to the top; two or three gallons at a time is plenty. (Any more than that, and it gets hard to work with the roller, not to mention heavy to lug around!) If you've got too much paint to mix all at once, just add and stir as room becomes available in the bucket.

   If you've bought paint in a 5-gallon bucket rather than in gallon cans, stir well, then pour a third or so of the contents into the empty bucket to give you enough room to insert the paint screen in the new bucket.

2. Hook the paint screen over the edge of your 5-gallon bucket, slide a roller cover on your roller, and screw on the handle extension. Roll the roller down the paint screen until it just begins to pick up some paint, then roll it down the dry part of the screen several more times to distribute the paint evenly and squeeze out some of the excess.

paint screen

3. The rule of thumb in painting is to start at the top and work down. Strap on a pair of goggles to protect your eyes, then pick one corner of the ceiling to start. Roll about a 3-foot by 3-foot section, then move along and do an adjoining section about the same size. Ceiling work is the most tiring part of this job — give your arms and neck a break every few minutes. Don't worry about getting paint all the way into the corners or right up close to any overhead light fixtures; we'll go back and cut in these areas in a minute.

4. Once the ceiling is done, start on the walls. Direction isn't critical when you're working with a roller, although I generally work up-and-down, and left-to-right. Just try to work in some semblance of a pattern, one area at a time. If the roller is leaving "tails," you may be overloading it with paint. (If you're getting excessive drips, you're DEFINITELY overloading it with paint!) You'll get the hang of things pretty quickly. Try to clean up drips and even out thick spots as you go along.

5. As you work the walls, don't try to get the roller too close to electrical outlets, door trim, or baseboards. Leave a comfortable 2 to 3 inches for cutting in with a brush later.

⚠ CAUTIONS & CAVEATS:

For safety's (and sanity's!) sake, keep kids and pets away from any area where you're trying to paint. And don't forget to open windows, grab a portable fan – do whatever you can to make sure your work area is well-ventilated.

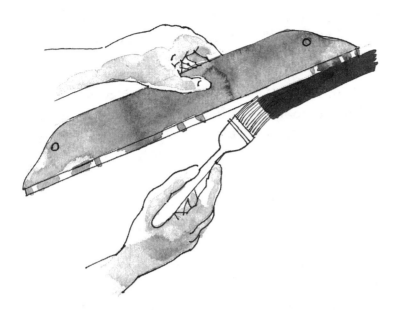

A metal-edged paint shield can help you protect critical areas.

6. Room all rolled? Go back and cut in the corners and edges with a brush. (You'll probably find it easier to work out of a gallon paint container or coffee can, rather than lugging the 5-gallon container around.)

Note: Some folks do their cutting in FIRST, before they roll the big areas. I've always found it easier to see exactly what needs to be cut in if I do it the other way 'round. And you get the instant gratification of LOTS of paint going on in a hurry!

7. Apply the semi-gloss paint to baseboard, trim and doors LAST. Clean your roller and roll the doors; use a (clean) brush for baseboards and trim. A metal-edged paint shield can help you cut in critical areas (close to the carpet, for example).

8. Let paint dry for at least an hour or so before pulling off masking paper. But don't wait TOO long or the adhesive on the back of the masking tape can leave a tacky mess!

Clean-up & Storage

Always follow the paint manufacturer's instructions for cleaning up rollers and brushes. Whether your paint allows water clean-up or requires a solvent, don't put it off — if you want to salvage your utensils for another painting job, it's best to take care of them as soon as possible after you finish.

If you're just taking a break for lunch, stow paint brushes and rollers inside a plastic food storage bag so they don't dry out while you're gone. I've even wrapped an entire roller tray in a large plastic garbage bag to save clean-up during a short absence, but beware — it's all too easy to forget what's UNDER that lumpy black plastic and step on it by mistake! That's the voice of experience you hear moaning in the background.

For long-term storage, keep leftover paint in its original can so you'll remember the exact brand and type. It may sound obvious, but it took me a while to learn: clean off the lip of the can thoroughly before tapping the lid back in place and you'll get a much better (and more airtight) fit.

Use a felt-tipped permanent marking pen to write the date and the room painted (East bedroom, 11/97) on the can lid for easy reference.

> **TIP:**
> Got a cathedral ceiling, open stairwell, or other high spot you can't reach, even with the roller handle extension fully telescoped? Some painting supply and equipment rental stores will let you rent scaffolding by the day for a nominal price.

Sticky Patio Doors

Ideally, sliding glass patio doors glide easily along their lower track. When doors don't roll smoothly, often the problem is simply due to an accumulation of dust, dirt, and rocks in that lower channel. Use a small screwdriver or toothbrush and small vacuum attachment to gently remove any grit and debris. A dab of bar soap in the channel once it's clean may help things roll more smoothly. (DON'T use an oil-based lubricant, as grease will tend to collect and trap grit and dirt.)

If the problem seems to be limited to one particular section where the door "binds," and there doesn't seem to be a rock or other obstruction in the channel, examine the track closely for dents and dings. You may be able to gently straighten the metal track by tweaking it with a pair of pliers, but in most cases a serious deformity means the track will need to be replaced (often no small job!).

Another potential source of sticky-door problems is the rollers themselves. If they're simply out of alignment, it may be possible to adjust their height by turning a screw — check the edge and face of the door for an access hole. Rocks and grit can also chew up the plastic roller wheels over time.

If the rollers need to be replaced, you'll need to remove the doors from the track to reach the mounting screws. ENLIST A STRONG HELPER for this one; it's usually a two-person job. For most patio doors, lift straight up, then angle the bottom of the door outward so the rollers clear the track. Sometimes it helps to retract the rollers a bit by turning the

height-adjustment screw. A few models have breaks in the lower track that allow the wheels to exit the track only in a certain position.

Unscrew the old rollers and, if you are lucky enough to find a label with the door's manufacturer and model number, jot down that information. Bring the old parts and manufacturer information with you to the hardware store to ensure that the replacements you buy will be compatible.

Hanging Miniblinds

For an inexpensive window-covering, nothing beats vinyl miniblinds. They go up quickly, take tremendous abuse, and (except on close inspection) look much the same as more costly metal blinds.

Vinyl miniblinds come in a range of standard sizes rather than being custom-crafted for your window — one of the reasons manufacturers are able to keep the price down. Since windows tend to come in standard sizes, too, there's probably a stock miniblind that comes close.

Measure your window, noting the total distance inside the window well, not just the glass size. Write down the WIDTH first (measuring at the TOP, where the blind will be mounted), then the length.

One of the beauties of vinyl blinds is that the top rail can be trimmed by up to an inch or so if a stock width is not a perfect fit. So if your window happens to be 45 1/2 inches wide, buy a standard 46-inch blind and plan to shave a 1/4 inch off each end.

Here are the tools & materials you'll need to get started:

Phillips screwdriver or, better yet, a screw gun
measuring tape
1-inch drywall or other sturdy Phillips-head screws
hacksaw with fine-toothed blade
scissors
pencil

1. Open the box that contains the miniblind, and pull out the packet of mounting brackets and screws. Keep the brackets, but throw out the screws. They're usually junk.

2. Double-check the width measurement at the top of the window, then deduct 1/8 to 1/4 inch from the total window width to allow for clearance. Now stretch the tape along the top rail of the miniblind. Is the rail just a tad too long? You can trim off up to about one inch total (1/2 inch on each end). Split the difference so it doesn't all come off one end.

   Use a hacksaw with a fine-toothed blade, and saw away. Just be certain not to cut so close to the mechanism that you won't have room for the end of the blind to fit into the mounting bracket.

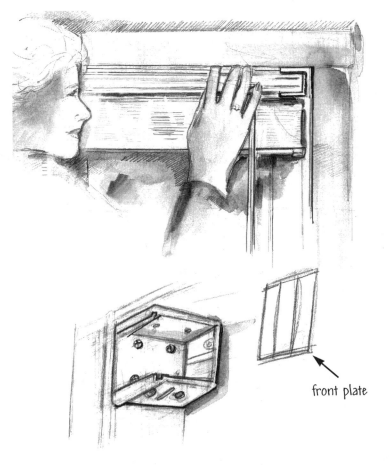

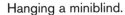
front plate

Hanging a miniblind.

CAUTIONS & CAVEATS:

Until fairly recently, some vinyl miniblinds contained lead. Most manufacturers have now re-formulated their blinds, but (particularly if you have young children or pregnant women in your household), you may want to test any older vinyl miniblinds in your house for possible lead content.

3. Take a look at the mounting brackets that came with the miniblind. They will look like little plastic cubes with holes in them. Slide out the front retaining plates (one of the walls of the cube).

4. Hold one bracket in the upper left corner of the window opening, and position it so that the RIGHT edge of the cube is open to allow the blind to slide into place. (That is, the cube will have "walls" on the top, bottom, back, and left sides.)

5. Push the cube's left side snug up against the window well, and scoot it so it sits recessed back just about a 1/2 inch inside the well. With a pencil, mark the 2 small holes up inside the top wall.

   If you've positioned the bracket correctly, there should be large holes on the BOTTOM of the cube, and SMALL holes on the top. If your configuration is the opposite, you've either got the cube upside down, or you're using the wrong bracket. Some manufacturers make them interchangeable, in which case you'll have BOTH small AND large holes on each end.

6. Here's the hard part. You need to screw the bracket in place at the position marked.

   If you're really, REALLY good with a screw gun, you may be able to hold the bracket with one hand, balance a screw on the end of the gun, and give it a whirl. Otherwise, start the screw at the pencil mark WITHOUT the bracket in place, at first. Then when you've got a good hole started, back the screw out, replace the bracket, and go again. An even easier method is to drill a small pilot hole with a 1/8-inch drill bit first. Got the idea? Okay, mount both brackets (far left and far right), using two screws each.

7. Enlist a helper to help you check to see if the miniblind will slide properly into place in the two brackets. Trim another 1/8 inch or so off the top rail, if necessary.

8. Got the blind up and in place? Have your helper hold it there or, better yet, slip the little plastic retaining plates back into the brackets to make sure the blind doesn't pull out as you're working.

9. Depending on the width of the blind, you'll generally have one or two metal L-shaped brackets that help support it in the middle. (Very narrow blinds won't come with a middle bracket.) The tab in the metal bracket fits into a little groove or slot cut in the BOTTOM of the miniblind's top rail.

   Look closely to see exactly where these slots are located; then mark the top window well with your pencil so you'll know where to attach the metal support brackets.

10. Remove the plastic retaining plates from the end brackets, and have your helper assist you in taking down the blind again. Screw the metal support brackets into place at the spots you marked. (Remember to set them back far enough into the window well so that the tab can slip into the miniblind's groove.)

11. Put the blind back up and check the fit. If everything's positioned correctly, the metal supports will snap into place in the grooves. Slide the plastic retaining plates back into the end brackets to keep the blind in position, and slip the twirler rod over the hook near the left-hand bracket.

12. Lower the blind all the way. If the slats are a tad too long to fit inside the window opening, trim the horizontal slats with scissors. If necessary, also remove the endcaps and trim the thick bottom slat using a hacksaw. Then replace the caps.

> **TIP:**
> Particularly when using drywall screws, it's important to "snug up" the screws. If the heads protrude too far into the bracket opening, it will be tough to fit the miniblind rail into place.

13. You can also remove slats to adjust the blind's overall length. This is unnecessary on smaller-width windows, unless you object to having the extra slats bunch up at the bottom. But it IS important to adjust the length on wider blinds, to avoid the excess weight of all those extra slats which can stress and even crack the upper rail when you pull on the raise-and-lowering string.

To shorten a miniblind, mark the last slat you want to KEEP with a piece of tape. Remove the blind from its brackets, and stretch it out on the floor. Pull the little plugs out of the bottom slat and cut the knots out of the strings. Remove the excess slats and cut the thread-like webbing (but NOT the heavier pull-strings) back to several ladder-holes longer than the slat you marked. Slip the thick bottom slat into the ladder rung just below the last slat, rethread the strings into the (small) top holes of the thicker bottom slat, and re-knot. Tuck the webbing ends neatly inside the (large) bottom holes, then replace the plugs.

> **TIP:**
> Okay, okay – that "rethreading" step is a little trickier than it sounds. Use a miniature screwdriver or large nail to help poke the string through.

Vinyl Floor Tile

Vinyl floor tile (sometimes called "resilient flooring") comes in two basic formats — *tile squares,* one-foot square pieces, usually with a self-adhesive backing; and *sheet flooring,* manufactured in 6-foot and 12-foot wide rolls and typically set in place with a troweled-on adhesive.

Laying new vinyl tile is a breeze compared with ripping up whatever old material is on the floor and prepping the surface to accept the new material. So before we talk about a whole new floor, let's start with some of the *easier* repairs.

Replacing a Damaged Tile Square

If only one or two tile squares are damaged, it's a fairly simple matter to pull them up and replace them. With any luck, your tile pattern will still be available. Check around at various hardware and flooring stores. (If there's nothing remotely resembling your tile pattern still on the market, maybe it's time for new flooring anyway!)

To soften the tile's adhesive and make removal easier, heat the damaged square with a blow-dryer or lay a thin, soft cloth over the top of the tile and rub gently with an iron set on medium heat.

Use a putty knife to pry up the defective tile, being careful not to damage adjacent tiles as you do so. If necessary, use a razor knife to cut the damaged tile into two or more pieces, and remove one piece at a time.

Scrape as much of the old adhesive out of the vacant spot as possible; it's important that the surface where you'll set the new tile is clean and perfectly smooth. If necessary, daub a little adhesive remover or solvent on a clean rag, and gently wipe

> ⚠ **CAUTIONS & CAVEATS:**
> Older tile may contain asbestos. When in doubt, have an expert evaluate the composition of your old tile before beginning. Do NOT attempt to remove any tile yourself that might contain asbestos.

up any excess adhesive (but be careful NOT to get solvent on or under adjoining tiles!)

Before you set the new tile in place, look to see if there's an orientation that makes a difference in the floor's pattern. Also check the fit before you remove the paper backing (for self-adhesive tiles) or spread adhesive (for glue-in-place tiles). Occasionally it may be necessary to trim the new tile slightly.

> **TIP:**
> To help ensure that self-adhesive tiles stick firmly, set them in the sun or a warm part of the house for an hour or so before peeling off the backing.

Fit okay? For self-adhesive tiles, remove the paper backing. For trowelled-adhesive tiles, carefully spread a thin layer of a compatible tile adhesive with a serrated trowel, being careful not to smudge adhesive on adjoining tile. Set the new tile in place and push down firmly.

Patching Sheet Vinyl

One unsightly tear or burn in sheet vinyl doesn't necessarily mean you have to rip out and replace the entire floor. Often, the bad spot can be patched so the repair is hardly noticeable.

You'll need a piece of matching vinyl slightly larger than the area to be replaced. If the contractor who installed the floor didn't happen to leave a few extra scraps lying around (check your basement, attic, and under sinks), you may be able to pilfer a piece from under the refrigerator or another inconspicuous location.

Cut a patch that's 1 to 2 inches larger than what you need. Lay the patch over the bad spot, making sure you match the

patterns. Tape the patch firmly in place with wide masking or electrician's tape.

Put a *fresh blade* in your razor knife. This is one time when sharpness really makes a difference. Then, pressing firmly through BOTH layers of vinyl tile, cut the patch to size, using a metal straight-edge as a guide. If possible, follow a line in the pattern to help conceal the cut.

Gently pull off the tape and set the patch aside. Carefully remove the damaged section of tile and clean off excess adhesive (see directions above). Lay the patch in place, and check the fit. Trim with scissors or razor knife if necessary.

Using a notched trowel, spread a thin layer of adhesive in the area to be patched. (For very small patches, you may want to apply the adhesive to the back of the patch itself.) Fit the patch into place, and carefully wipe away any excess adhesive.

Weigh the patch down with a heavy object to hold it in place until the adhesive is thoroughly dry. Fill in any gaps with colored caulk.

Removing Old Flooring

Sometimes, however, a simple repair is not enough. Could it be time to redo the entire floor?

Some books will tell you it's okay to lay new vinyl flooring down on top of the existing floor, provided the old material is still sound and well-adhered. That's certainly the easier way to go, but in my humble opinion, you'll get a better result if you take the time to do it right. Go ahead and remove the old floor tile first.

Now I'll admit, ripping up old linoleum is one of those chores for which the term "sweat equity" was invented. But even more than a strong pair of biceps (although those help), you'll need an abundant supply of time and patience.

Here are the tools & materials you'll need to get started:

hammer
flat prybar
putty knife
razor knife
lacquer thinner
paper towels
Fix-All or similar patching compound
sanding block and paper

1. Using your putty knife, hammer, and prybar, gently remove the baseboard or shoe molding covering the edges of the old flooring material. Since these pieces are already cut to fit, it's easiest if you can save and re-use them. Number the pieces for future reference. If there is a metal threshold strip at the doorway, remove the screws or nails holding it in place and pull it up as well.

2. Starting in one corner, see if you can pry up an edge of the flooring material. Sometimes you'll get lucky and the mate-

! CAUTIONS & CAVEATS:

As noted above, older floor tile may contain asbestos. When in doubt, have a professional determine the composition of the old flooring before you begin. If asbestos is present, this is definitely a time to **call in an expert!** Do NOT attempt to remove old asbestos tile yourself.

rial will zip right off. Most of the time it won't be nearly that simple.

3. Scrape the old flooring material up, a section at a time, working the putty knife back and forth under the edge. If necessary, dab or pour a little lacquer thinner or other adhesive remover near the edge of the tile to see if that makes the task any easier.

! CAUTIONS & CAVEATS:

Solvents are extremely flammable and the fumes can be hazardous to your health if you breathe them for any period of time. When working with solvents, always make sure you have good ventilation, keep solvents away from flames, and wear gloves and other protective clothing as recommended by the solvent manufacturer.

One alternative for removing old flooring from a concrete slab base is to cover a small area at a time with dry ice (check your telephone directory's yellow pages under "dry ice" for retailers). The extreme cold will shrink the tiles and pop them loose from the adhesive.

4. Use your putty knife and a solvent to scrape off as much of the old adhesive from the subfloor as possible. Fill any holes or irregularities in the subfloor with Fix-All or a similar patching compound, and sand the patches flat when dry. If the surface is really a mess, consider installing a 3/8-inch or 1/2-inch underlayment material over your existing subflooring material. You really do need a completely clean, flat surface for a good finished look to your new tile.

Is your floor all prepped and looking good? Okay! Next you'll need to decide which type of resilient flooring you want to install: tile squares or sheet vinyl.

Both have their advantages and disadvantages. *Tile squares* are simpler for beginners to install and if you have tenants (or kids!) who are tough on floors, squares make it fairly easy to pop out the damaged section and pop in a new tile or two. On the other hand, tile squares do have those inevitable seam lines which can collect dirt. *Sheet vinyl* is more awkward to install initially (particularly in rooms with lots of jogs and angles), but gives a more professional look once it's down and often wears better.

Installing Tile Squares

Most tile squares are one square foot in size. To buy the right amount, just total up the area of the room to be covered (length times width, remember?) and add 10% for cutting waste. (Since tiles are often boxed lots of 45, you'll probably wind up having to buy extra anyway.)

Here are the tools & materials you'll need to get started:

tape measure
chalk line
long carpenter's square
whisk broom and dustpan
vinyl tiles
razor knife

1. Our goal at the outset is to find the center of the room. Measure one edge of the room near the baseboard and mark its midpoint. Then locate the midpoint of the opposite edge.

2. Have a helper hold an end of your chalk line on one of your marks (or weigh it down firmly with a brick or other heavy object so that the string stays on the mark) while you pull the line taut across the second mark, and snap a line.

3. Do the same with the other two walls, and again snap a line between your marks. You should now have a chalk-marked "X" in the middle of the room. Use your square to see if the lines of the "X" are truly perpendicular. (Sometimes walls aren't perfectly square, which will throw your line off.)

4. Lay a test row of tiles along what seems to be your straightest coordinate from the center of the floor all the way to both walls. (Don't remove the paper backing for now; we're just checking to see how the pattern will fall.)

Since life isn't perfect, invariably you'll have room for only *part* of a tile on each edge. Adjust the row if necessary to equalize the gap. Half a tile on each edge is ideal. *Note:* Tiny sections of tile are hard to cut. If you wind up with skinny little borders of just an inch or two, move the starting point of your row over 6 inches.

> **TIP:**
> For best adhesion, make sure your boxes of tile are room temperature before you begin. (Don't leave them in a cold garage overnight!)

5. Once your first test row has been adjusted, lay a second test row along the other arm of your "X," starting from the center. Again, adjust the rows to equalize the gaps at both edges. Carefully mark the new position of your center tile.

6. Now that your layout has been adjusted, snap a revised chalk line. (Just measure the number of inches you have moved the center tile off the original line, then snap a parallel line that same number of inches over.) Smudge or "x"-out the original chalk line so you don't get confused.

7. To lay out a precise perpendicular line in the center, use a long metal carpenter's square, then snap a corresponding chalk line. (Check your layout with a tape measure. Measure 3 feet along one axis and 4 feet along the other. The hypotenuse between those two points should measure 5 feet if you've got a perfect right triangle.)

8. Clear your work area and use your whisk broom and dustpan to make sure your starting point is perfectly clean and grit-free. Pull the paper backing off your first piece of tile, and examine the back for a directional arrow. It really doesn't matter what direction you choose, but you'll want to set all the tiles in the same way.

Carefully place the first tile along the lines you've marked. The first tile is always the most critical, since it will determine the lay of all the others, so take your time and get it right. The glue on self-adhesive tile tends to be pretty aggressive, so you won't have a lot of "play" once you set the tile down.

9. Working along your longest axis, lay another 4 or 5 tiles, butting them tight against one another. Use your whisk broom as you go along to make sure the surface is grit-free before you set each tile. To help keep the edges in a straight line, use a straight-edge or carpenter's square as a guide.

Ideally, the tile edges will precisely follow your chalked line. Once you set your first tile, however, you're committed and must follow the line dictated by the tile. A slight variation really won't make much difference in an average-sized room. If you find yourself deviating greatly from your chalk line after just 4 or 5 tiles, however, you may want to consider pulling them up and starting again.

10. Once you have your first row of 4 or 5 tiles down, go back to the center and lay a tile or two along the other axis. The important thing is to butt the tile edge *tightly* against the preceding tile, and align the gaps. Don't get too carried away laying tiles straight out along the second axis; as soon as possible, begin to fill in the "stair-step" tiles. Continue working from the middle outward until all the areas that take full tiles have been covered.

> **TIP:**
> For tiles in a heavy traffic areas or for narrow strips of tile at the edges of a room, consider adding a *thin* coat of multi-purpose flooring adhesive to the back of the tile as a little added insurance.

11. At doorways, the finished tile should reach to the middle of the opening. Be sure to cut the tile an inch or two longer to give the metal threshold (which will eventually go on top) plenty to hold onto for a firm grip.

12. You'll need to cut partial tiles to fill in around the perimeter of the room. You can, of course, simply measure the gap with a tape measure, and then cut a section of tile to fit.

An even easier way to transfer the needed dimension is to lay the tile to be cut (with its paper backing still on) exactly over the top of the next full tile BACK from the wall. Lay another tile (which you will be using as a marking guide) tight up against the wall so that its other edge overlaps the tile to be cut. Mark the line where the two tiles lap, and cut there. (To allow for variation in the wall, I usually nip off an additional 1/8 inch.) The piece still showing will be a perfect fit for the gap along the perimeter.

If you run into odd angles or curves, use thin cardboard, Kraft paper, or even shopping bag paper as a template to help you cut the tile accurately.

13. Finish up by re-installing the shoe molding or baseboard around the perimeter. Cover tile edges at doorways with the metal threshold strip.

TIPS:

• The *proper* way to lay tile around a toilet is to completely lift the fixture off its mounting so the tile can go underneath. With tile squares, however, you can cheat a little bit. As long as you manage to get a relatively precise fit with your curved cuts, you can fill the remaining gap with a good tub-and-tile caulk and no one will ever know the difference.

• Start your perimeter "fill-in" pieces in the *middle* of a wall, and then work toward either edge.

• There's nothing more frustrating than trying to saw through vinyl floor tile with an old blade. Spring for a sharp, new blade or two for your razor knife before you begin.

• Use a piece of scrap lumber or plywood as a cutting board; *don't* cut your next piece of tile on top of the flooring you've already laid!

Installing Sheet Vinyl

I always hope there's no camera around when I'm trying to install sheet vinyl. While it might make a terrific entry for *America's Funniest Home Videos,* they'd have to bleep out more than a few expletives.

Directions for laying sheet vinyl usually start by blithely telling you to "gently unroll the vinyl, letting it curl up the edges of the room." In real life, maneuvering the vinyl into position (and trying to get it to STAY there) is like trying to align all eight tentacles of a wriggly octopus.

The job's not TOO bad if you've got a small, perfectly rectangular room. But any jogs or angles make it a much bigger challenge.

That's not to say you can't do it. You CAN. But be prepared for a certain amount of frustration. (And watch out for covert camera crews!)

Here are the tools & materials you'll need to get started:

sheet vinyl
weights (cement blocks or
 buckets of water)
scissors
vinyl adhesive
small-toothed trowel
whisk broom and dustpan
razor knife
rolling pin

1. Sheet vinyl comes in 6-foot and 12-foot rolls. If possible, buy enough to allow for a seamless installation. (Draw your room out on graph paper and take it with you to the flooring store if you need help deciding how much vinyl to buy.)

2. Vinyl is a lot easier to work with when it's warm, so plan ahead. Set the roll in the sun for a few hours before you begin, or lay the vinyl flat in your living room and cover it with an electric blanket to warm up. While the vinyl's warming, use your whisk broom to make sure the floor where you'll be working is clean.

3. Now comes the tough part. You'll need to trim the vinyl ALMOST to its final size in order to get it neatly "curling up the walls." But since walls often aren't perfectly square, you can't simply transfer the exact dimensions and cut.

Every situation is different, but in general it's easiest if you start with the longest wall. Lay the vinyl in place, with about 3 inches extra rolling up the wall on the long edge. To keep the vinyl from shifting while you work, weigh it down with cement blocks wrapped in old towels or buckets filled with water.

4. Cut your material ROUGHLY to the dimensions of the rest of the room, allowing somewhere between 3 and 6 extra inches of margin all around. Work slowly and carefully, making sure you take off ONLY what you need to remove to get the vinyl to lay flat. Try not to let the vinyl kink or tear (easier said than done!).

If your layout will require lots of jogs and angles, one alternative is to make a paper template that is the exact size and shape of the area to be covered. Use heavy Kraft paper, taping lengths of paper together with masking tape until you have a piece big enough to cover the area, and use scissors to trim it to size. Then tape the template firmly in place on your sheet vinyl and cut around the outline with a razor knife. If you're nervous about getting the size and shape exact, you can leave an extra 1/2 inch to 1 inch all around, although this may make it a little harder to get into place and will require extra cutting later.

TIP:
If you're working on a bathroom, have a handy friend or plumber help you remove the toilet before you start.

TIP:
Rather than try to cut vinyl precisely to fit around rounded door molding, shave off the bottom end of the molding with a fine-toothed hacksaw so the vinyl can slip underneath.

TIPS:
• If your room is too large for a single piece of vinyl, pick a spot along a line in the pattern for the seam. Match the patterns, and overlap your two pieces of material. Then cut through both pieces of vinyl at the same time, using a straight-edge as a guide.

• If your layout requires a seam, spread adhesive for the first section to within 6-12 inches of the seam's edge; then carefully roll back the edge and trowel about a 3-foot strip with adhesive — enough to grip the first couple of feet of the adjoining piece. You'll need to work quickly, however. If the adhesive on the first piece has set, it can be tough to lift its edge to get adhesive underneath. Be sure to weigh the seam area down until it has dried completely.

5. Once you've gotten the vinyl cut more or less to shape, use a straight-edge to guide your razor knife as you cut along the walls. Press the straight-edge hard into the corner to make sure you are cutting close to the wall.

Trim concave (inside) corners using a succession of gentle, scooping cuts (it usually takes less of a cut that you think, so work up to it slowly!)

For convex (outside) corners, make a vertical cut in the material at the corner. Here again, take it slow so you don't cut too far.

For curves (such as around the toilet drain) or odd angles, use lightweight cardboard or heavy paper to make a template.

> **TIP:**
> For a durable finish on seams OR to help repair those inevitable "oops" cuts, apply a thin coating of seam sealer (available at most carpet stores).

> **TIP:**
> If you discover air bubbles when you're done, don't panic. Give it a day or so. If the vinyl doesn't settle into place, prick the bubble with a pin and press down firmly. For larger air-pockets, slit (preferably along a line in the pattern so it won't show), and use a small putty knife or a nail to force a little extra adhesive in through the slit.

6. Got the vinyl cut to shape? Then the hard part's over with — now the fun begins!

To apply the adhesive, gently roll back half of the vinyl. (Again, weigh down the remaining half to make sure it doesn't shift in the process.)

Sweep the exposed floor with your whisk broom again, just to make certain you haven't tracked in any bits of sand and there are no vinyl trimmings in the way.

7. Working from the *center outward,* apply a thin coat of adhesive with a fine-toothed trowel. It may LOOK too thin to hold, but this stuff has an alligator's tenacity. The biggest mistake you can make here is to get it on too thick, which will give the finished surface a mushy, dimpled look.

8. Roll the vinyl into place on top of the adhesive and, working from the center out, go over it with a rolling pin to try to get all the air bubbles out. Once the first half is firmly in place, move your weights over to the side you just put down, and do the other half. (Just remember to work the adhesive from the center of the room toward the edges.)

9. Finish by reinstalling shoe molding or baseboards around the perimeter, and by re-attaching metal threshold strips at doorways.

Ceramic Tile

Although more expensive than vinyl flooring or laminate countertops, ceramic tile adds a touch of glamour to baths and kitchens that's usually well worth the difference in price.

Treated right, ceramic tile should give you years of service. Occasionally, however, repairs may be necessary. Here are some tips for two of the most common repairs: re-grouting ceramic tile, and replacing a cracked or broken tile.

Re-Grouting Tile

The key to a good grout repair is to get as much of the old grout out as possible. Use a specialized tool called a grout saw or, if the existing grout seems to be distintegrating in several small sections, try removing the pieces with an ice pick or miniature screwdriver. Be careful not to damage adjacent tile (or, of course, your fingers!).

Mix up a small amount of similar-colored grout to about the consistency of toothpaste. (You should be able to pick up a small container of plain old white or grey grout at any hardware store. Your local tile store will also have a good selection of colored grouts to choose from, if necessary.)

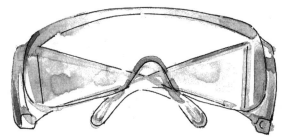

Use goggles to protect your eyes as you chip out broken tile.

For large-scale re-grouting jobs, use a float to work the grout into the newly-opened grout lines. For smaller grout repairs, you can just use your finger. Wipe the tiles clean with a damp sponge or rag. Let the grout dry *thoroughly* — at least 24 hours — before using.

Replacing a Cracked or Broken Tile

To replace one tile that's cracked or broken, score around the tile along the grout line with an inexpensive glass cutting tool. Then cut an "X" from corner to corner of the damaged tile.

Cover your work area with a drop cloth or old towel to keep chips from scratching nearby surfaces or clogging the drain.

Wearing goggles to protect your eyes, chip gently at the center of the broken tile, using a hammer and cold chisel. Your goal is to crack the tile neatly along the scored line, without damaging adjacent tiles. Once the tile breaks, lift out the pieces with a putty knife, and remove as much of the old mortar or tile adhesive as possible.

A good tile store may be able to locate a tile for you that's a passable match. If you can't seem to find anything close, try going a little wild — use a patterned tile or contrasting color as a decorative accent.

To install the new tile, mix up a small amount of thinset mortar and apply it to the back of the tile with a notched trowel. (How much you put on and how finely-toothed the trowel should be will depend on the thickness you're trying to match.) Fit the tile gently into place, and use a level or other straight-edge to help you match the surrounding surfaces as closely as possible. Use a nail or miniature screwdriver to remove any excess mortar from grout lines and tiles. Let the mortar dry for 24 hours before attempting to grout the new tile.

> **TIP:**
> If the tile is on a vertical surface such as the wall of a shower, use duct or adhesive tape to hold the tile in place until it dries.

Laying New Ceramic Tile

Got the urge to try your hand at laying new ceramic tile? It's a mud-pie kind of project... lots of fun if you don't mind getting dirty.

When you purchase tile, be sure to buy the right type for the job you have in mind — some tiles are made expressly for floor, wall, or countertop applications, while others are multi-purpose.

Tile is expensive, so bring the dimensions of your project area with you and get professional assistance in choosing the right number of field, trim, and bullnose edging tiles. They'll undoubtedly factor in cutting-waste as well. Before you leave the store with your precious cargo, ask the clerk to open any sealed boxes so you can check for cracks or breakage.

There is one catch to ceramic tile work that could require you to **call in an expert** — you'll need to make sure the surface you'll be working on is properly prepared for tile. For countertops, you'll need a stout (approximately 3/4-inch) layer of plywood topped by cement backer board. Around tubs and showers, you'll usually want to use cement board over a water-resistant type of

Use a notched trowel to apply thinset mortar.

drywall known as "green board." Before you set floor tile, you may need additional plywood to stiffen the surface, depending on the type of subfloor already in place. Some manufacturers recommend installing a layer of felt over the subfloor. And for wet applications (shower floors, for example), a waterproofing membrane may be necessary.

Have a carpenter or experienced tile person evaluate your existing surfaces and add plywood and other tile backing as necessary.

Here are the tools & materials you'll need to get started:

tape measure
notched trowel
thinset or mastic
acrylic admix
spacers
float
putty knife
level or scrap of 2 x 4
tile saw (you may be able to rent one from your tile
   store)

tile nippers	sponge
tile	clean, soft rags
grout	grout sealer

A couple of words about tools and materials before we begin. For a small job, or if you're just beginning and have plenty of time, you can buy an inexpensive mechanical tile cutter. These work by scoring the surface of the tile with a blade, and provide a guide to help you snap the tile in two along the score mark. If you're doing any amount of tile work, however, rent a good electric (wet) tile saw at your local tile store. Ask the store to show you exactly how to use the saw, and be sure you understand its safety features.

Whether you choose thinset mortar or mastic will depend upon the manufacturer's recommendations and perhaps your own preferences. Personally, I've been happier with the long-term results using thinset. If you do decide to use thinset, remember that it should be mixed with a liquid acrylic adhesive rather than with plain water. Your hardware or tile store should be able to point you to the right stuff.

1. The most critical part about setting tile is laying it out well to start. In general, you'll want to begin with whole tiles at the edge of countertops that jut into rooms. For floors, use the layout tips given above for laying vinyl tile squares to help you align your pattern. Whatever your project, lay out a test row or two to help you gauge your margins and make sure you have the look you're after.

2. Using a notched trowel, apply a layer of thinset mortar mixed to the consistency of toothpaste OR apply pre-mixed mastic. Lay each tile with a firm set-and-twist motion to settle it uniformly into the grout. Check the level of each tile compared to its neighbor with a level or a length of 2 x 4, wrapped in cloth to protect the tile's surface.

3. Keep your working area relatively small (2 or 3 square feet) so that you'll have time to place and adjust the tiles before your adhesive begins to set up. Use tile spacers between tiles to help you maintain an even spacing distance.

4. For partial tiles, cut using a tile saw. (You may want to wait to apply the mortar or mastic until you've already cut the partial tiles to fit, as individually crafting them can be time-consuming.)

5. Once the tiles have all been set, *gently* clean excess mortar from tile surfaces and grout lines using a nail or miniature screwdriver. Wait an hour or two and then pull spacers out using needlenose pliers or a nail, being careful not to inadvertently dislodge a tile. (If one or two spacers are especially recalcitrant, just let them stay.) Clean up your tools, and clean and save spacers for future use. Let the tile set up for a day before attempting to grout it.

6. When you're ready to grout, again use acrylic admix to mix your grout to a consistency of cooked cereal. Use the edge of your float to coax the grout into seams, working across the surface in various directions. When all the grout lines are nicely filled, scrape as much excess grout off your working surface as possible with the float; then wipe carefully with a barely-damp sponge, being careful not to gouge the grout out of the seams.

7. Let the surface stand for 20 minutes or so, then go back with a soft, dry rag and remove as much of the filmy haze as possible from the tile's surface. Again, be careful not to gouge the grout.

8. When the grout is fully dry (give it a day or so), polish again with a soft cloth. Follow manufacturer's instructions for applying a grout sealer. (You may need to wait as much as a month to allow the grout to fully cure.) To keep grout in good condition, re-apply sealer as directed on the label.

Stand back and enjoy!

Installing Closet Organizers

Are disorganized closets one of your pet peeves? You don't need to be a master carpenter to install today's modular closet-organizer systems. There are a variety of good-looking, durable "do-it-yourself" systems available utilizing components made of coated wire or laminated particleboard.

Wire storage systems usually include a range of shelving options, from those designed to handle lightweight linen items to heavy-duty storage shelving. The wire components are generally fairly strong despite their light weight, and offer excellent ventilation.

Pre-drilled particleboard units typically combine strength and durability with more of a built-in look. While it may be tempting to try to "mix and match" components, you're usually better off to stick with one manufacturer's system to ensure that everything works together as it should.

Don't make your decision based on a snazzy brochure — check out the manufacturer's display in person at your hard-

Decide exactly what you'll want your closet to accommodate before beginning.

ware store. Examine the materials and hardware of each model closely, and don't hesitate to put baskets and drawer units to the "hands-on" test before making up your mind.

Once you've chosen a closet system you like, draw a scale model of your existing closet space and inventory its contents to help you decide which type of organizer will be most helpful and efficient. A series of low baskets in a child's closet, for example, may be handy for stashing toys or school supplies, while an over-and-under double-rod arrangement can maximize hanging space for shirts, blouses and slacks.

Each manufacturer's products assemble and install a little differently, so read the directions that come with your unit carefully.

Wire Organizers

Here are the tools & materials you'll need to get started:

> **level**
> **stepladder**
> **drill and 1/4-inch drill bit**
> **tape measure**
> **hammer**
> **screwdriver**

Wire units usually require you to install a row of shelf clips along the back wall of your closet, about a foot apart. (Use a level to help line them up straight.) These clips contain their own molly-type anchor mechanism that spreads inside the wall when you tighten the screw to hold firmly against the drywall.

The shelf snaps into the row of clips along the back, and then mounts to the side walls of the closet with end brackets. (To attach the end brackets to the wall, drill 1/4-inch holes and insert plastic wall anchors, then simply attach the end brackets with screws.)

Wire shelf units come in various lengths but can be cut to fit your existing space using a hacksaw or bolt cutters (you'll need to cut the shelf a little short to allow space for the end-brackets; follow the manufacturer's directions for exact allowance). Shorter shelves can be supported with a triangulating brace on one end rather than going wall-to-wall, if you choose. Braces will also be needed every 3 feet or so to help support longer shelves. Braces are typically mounted with plastic wall anchors and screws.

⚠ **CAUTIONS & CAVEATS:**

If you plan to load shelves with heavy items it's a good idea to mount the supporting brackets directly to a stud, if possible. Follow manufacturer's directions and ask about weight limitations.

Laminated Particleboard Organizers

Pre-drilled for easy assembly, particleboard organizer units require only a screwdriver and perhaps a hammer to put together.

Once assembled, tall units should be mounted to the wall with metal L-brackets for stability. You'll need to drill small pilot holes in the wall and the organizer unit, insert plastic anchors in the wall, and fasten the bracket in place with screws — piece of cake.

Some units are designed to hang from a wooden strip or "cleat" attached to the wall of your closet. If such a strip isn't already in place behind your existing closet rod, you'll need to purchase a length of 1 x 4, locate studs in the wall using a studfinder, and screw the strip in place to support the hanging unit.

TIP:

Tired of saggy closet rods, but can't bear to toss any of those vintage dresses? (They're bound to come back into fashion someday, right?) As a temporary measure, try replacing that old wooden dowel with an equivalent length of 1/2-inch or 3/4-inch galvanized plumbing pipe.

For a more professional look, break down and buy a triangular metal support bracket (or two!) designed to help brace your existing wooden dowel. Install a 1 x 4 wooden cleat or extend the existing cleat vertically, if necessary, to provide backing for the metal bracket. Be sure to attach cleats securely to the wall studs.

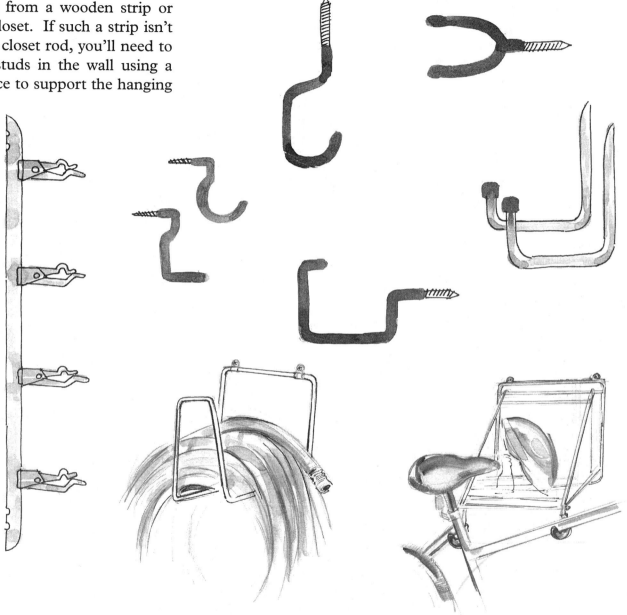

Garage organizers can help you neatly store bicycles, skis, garden equipment and more.

Getting the "Squeak" Out of Door Hinges

Is a squeaky door hinge driving you crazy? Surprisingly, an all-purpose household oil may NOT be the best answer. Oil acts like a magnet for household dust and dirt, so before long those hinges could be a mucky mess.

Silicone sprays or penetrating lubricants that contain teflon will probably do the job, at least temporarily. The liquid medium in the spray will evaporate, so you shouldn't have a problem with the hinge collecting dirt. (Since these are "wet" lubricants, you may want to hold a paper towel under the hinge as you spray to catch the excess.)

For long-term squeak squelching, however, graphite is the tried-and-true old stand-by. Powdered (dry) graphite comes in a handy little squeeze bottle. Just loosen the hinge pin (tap up with a flat-bladed screwdriver), pour a little of the fine graphite powder around the shaft; then re-seat the pin and work the door back and forth a number of times to distribute the powder. There are also a variety of graphited lock fluids that make it even easier to get the graphite to penetrate. Again, use a tissue or paper towel to wipe up any excess liquid.

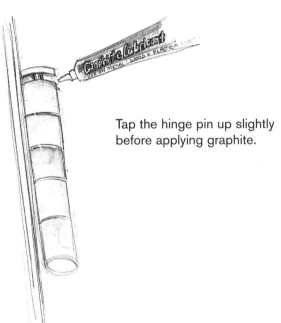

Tap the hinge pin up slightly before applying graphite.

Chapter 4

KIDS' PROJECTS

Or "HEY MOM, GUESS WHAT JOEY JUST DID . . ."

Let's face it, there's a certain inevitable "oops" quotient in life — especially with kids around the house. Luckily, most household horror stories are fixable with a few nails, a little glue, and a dab of spot remover. (Well, at least until your not-quite-angels start to drive, when those "oops"es may require the tender mercies of an auto body shop.)

Here are a few tips for coping with some of the most common kid-related fix-its.

Out, Out Damn Spot

Today's advanced spot removers are a great example of the "better living through chemistry" that your high school science teacher used to preach about. You'll find a selection of products designed for challenges like removing chewing gum and candle wax (not to mention run-of-the-mill carpet stains) at your hardware store.

I've also had great luck with the industrial-strength cleaning and spot-removal products sold for use by janitorial services. (If the professionals use it, I figure that's a pretty good sign!) One of my favorite all-purpose products is a janitorial liquid degreaser affectionately known around our house as "that pink stuff." Not only does it make short work of grease (even the really awful gunk that builds up on the filter in your range hood), but it earned my undying gratitude by removing an assortment of "mystery spots" left by careless tenants in expensive, light-colored berber carpeting.

Pets

Most kids seem to go through an "I just have to have a puppy" stage at some point in their young lives. If you've been wringing your hands over the fate of your rugs and furniture, relax — there have also been some major scientific advances in pet stain and odor removers in recent years. Many of my dog-owning friends swear by the new enzyme products. Check the shelves at your local pet or hardware stores, or ask at a janitorial supply house. Your veterinarian may also carry (or be able to recommend) an effective formulation.

⚠ **CAUTIONS & CAVEATS:**

Always follow label directions when using any spot or stain remover, especially the part about testing in an inconspicuous area before spritzing it in the dead center of your priceless Persian rug!

Colorful Catastrophes

Got a preschool Piccasso who views every wall as a fresh canvas? Try coaxing crayon "art" off wallpaper by heating (gently!) with a blow-dryer, then wiping with a paper towel. (Don't overheat or you might damage the wallpaper.) Or look for one of the new graffiti-removing sprays. Some formulations remove not only crayon but also lipstick, nail polish, and even permanent marker from carpet, wood, or brick. (Be sure to test in an inconspicuous spot first!) For painted walls, however, your best bet is to coat that magnum opus with a primer-sealer and brush on a little touch-up paint.

Patching Holes

There's a nice, round, fist-sized dent in the drywall of our guest bedroom. I'm not sure quite how it happened but it materialized the same weekend that a teenage relative came to visit, and I do recall plenty of good-natured elbowing and punching with the kid down the street. I sighed and hung a picture over it.

That's one solution. But it's really a pretty simple matter to fix most dings, dents, and holes in the wall. Here's what's involved:

Nail Holes & Nail Pops

Ordinary holes — the kind left from tacking up posters or nails holding that Certificate of Achievement — can be filled with a dab of lightweight spackle. You'll probably find that a finger works as well or better than a putty knife.

Nail pops (where the head of a drywall nail begins to show) are usually caused by either (a) drywall nails that missed the stud, or (b) studs that bowed away from the drywall as they dried. Either way, the nail isn't securely attached, and the normal expansion, contraction, and settling of your house causes the nailhead to work its way out of the drywall a bit. Just spackling over the popped nailhead won't fix the problem; it will more than likely reappear before long.

Using a studfinder to be sure you know exactly where the stud is located, secure the drywall to the stud with a new drywall screw an inch or two above or below the popped nail. Then use a nailset and hammer to give the offending nail a firm rap. You're not trying to drive it halfway across the continent; hit it just hard enough to sink the nailhead 1/8 inch or so into the drywall. Then use a putty knife and fill the dent with spackle. Let dry and then sand it smooth.

When Attila the Hun Was Here

For *monstrous* holes (bigger than 5 inches in diameter), check to be sure there are no underlying moisture or structural problems before you try to fix the hole. The proper repair approach will depend on whether you have drywall or plaster walls.

With *drywall,* use a razor knife or serrated drywall knife to cut out the damaged section. Enlarge the hole into a square or oblong section, cutting until you have uncovered a stud on either side.

CAUTIONS & CAVEATS:

When cutting drywall, be careful not to cut or nick electrical wiring inside the wall!

Remove the existing drywall back to the middle of each stud, leaving about an inch of wood uncovered where you can nail the new piece in place. Measure the hole, and cut a patch that's about 1/8-inch smaller all around. (You may be able to obtain scraps of drywall if you know someone doing new construction. Otherwise, just purchase a sheet of drywall from your local hardware store — it's pretty inexpensive. Either way, be sure to ask for drywall that's the same thickness as what you're replacing.)

Drill pilot holes in the edges of the drywall patch and hammer in place with drywall nails OR use an electric screw gun and drywall screws to attach the patch to the exposed studs. Apply a thin coat of joint compound around the four edges of the patch, then cover it with a strip of paper drywall tape.

Crisscross the area with fiberglass webbing tape, then apply a thin layer of joint compound.

Dings & Dents

Use spackle (for drywall) or patching plaster (for plaster walls) to fill smallish holes or indentations of about 2 inches or less across. Apply as smooth a coat as possible using a mid-sized (4-inch or 6-inch) drywall knife. Let it dry and sand flat.

For more substantial problems (up to about 5 inches in diameter), clean any loose debris from the edges of the hole, then crisscross the damaged area with self-adhesive fiberglass webbing tape. Apply a preliminary layer of joint compound and let it dry. Fill in with another layer of joint compound to just below the surface of the wall, and again let it dry. Then finish with a smooth layer of spackle, wait til dry, and sand. Brush with a coat of primer before repainting.

Smooth on another layer of compound and let it dry. Then apply a finish coat of spackle or topping compound (a very fine drywall mud), and sand smooth when dry. (Be careful not to sand through the spackle and joint compound and into the tape.) Seal with a coat of primer; then touch up the paint.

For repairs to *plaster* walls, your approach will need to be a little different. Use a hammer and cold chisel to remove any loose pieces of plaster around the edge of the hole.

> ⚠ **CAUTIONS & CAVEATS:**
> Always wear safety glasses for chipping jobs because pieces can go flying!

Unless your kid is destined for greatness as a kick-boxer, the plaster's backing material (lath or a type of gypsum board) should still be intact. (For repairs where the plaster's backing material is gone, or if you suspect structural damage, **call in an expert!)** Dampen the area to be patched using a spray bottle of water (this helps minimize cracking as the patching plaster dries). Mix up dry patching plaster to about the consistency of sticky bread dough, and apply a first ("scratch") coat about a 1/2-inch thick. Use a nail to (as the name implies) scratch a series of lines or "X"s into the plaster before it dries, to help the next coat adhere.

Once the scratch coat has dried, repeat the same steps for a second layer. Again, let it dry. Use a wide (10-inch) drywall knife to apply a smooth final coat of joint compound. Let it dry and sand well. Apply a coat of primer before repainting.

Screen Repairs

Along with skinned knees, screen doors are a common summer casualty. If your screen door is one of the inexpensive, light-gauge aluminum variety, it frankly may not pay to attempt a repair — it's that "you get what you pay for" thing again. Assuming you've got a fairly substantial aluminum or wooden frame to work with, however, it's not that tough to keep bugs behind bars.

Here are the tools & materials you'll need to get started:

new screen material
razor knife
tape measure

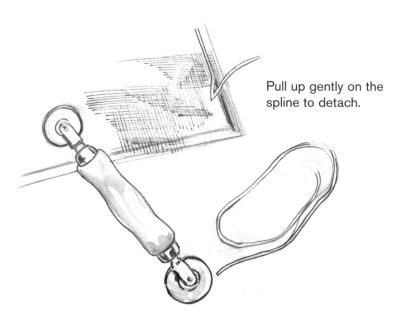

Pull up gently on the spline to detach.

for wooden frames:

putty knife
hammer
cutting-end nippers
staple gun and staples
scrap 1 x 4 or 2 x 4 lumber
C-clamps
small finish nails or brads

OR for aluminum frames:

vinyl spline material
spline roller

1. To remove the screening material in wooden doors, use a putty knife, hammer, and/or cutting-end nippers to *carefully* remove the strips of molding and all tacks or staples holding the screen in place. (Try not to damage the molding, as you'll need to reinstall it later!)

Choosing Screen Material

The two most common choices in screening material are fiberglass and aluminum mesh. Metal screen material tends to stand up a bit more to rough treatment, but it's also harder to work with and subject to corrosion. Fiberglass screening won't corrode, but tends to be not quite as durable as the metal screen material. If you opt for fiberglass, fold the material over along the edges to give a double-thickness for strength before you staple.

For aluminum door frames, look for the end of the plastic spline (a fat plastic thread squeezed into a groove in the frame to hold the screen in place). Lift up the end of the spline with an icepick or miniature screwdriver, then pull to detach the spline, releasing the screen all the way around.

2. That part's usually easy enough. But as anyone who's tried to fix a screen knows only too well, the real trick is getting the new material stretched taut — and HOLDING it that way as you replace the staples or spline.

Begin by cutting a new piece of screening material large enough to allow about a 1-inch overlap all the way around the opening in the door. (Use the old screen as a template if you like.)

3. If you have a wooden frame, staple the new screening along one of the *narrow* ends of the frame. Create a gentle bow in the wooden frame by propping each end up an inch or two with a piece of lumber; then hold the sides tight to your work table with C-clamps. (You can get the same effect by laying the frame flat on a concrete driveway with a 2 x 4 under each end, and then asking a helper to push down gently on the side rails.) Remember, you want a GENTLE bow in the frame, not a major bend.

With the frame bowed slightly, staple the screening to the other narrow end of the frame. Then remove the clamps or have your helper release the pressure, and let the frame straighten — tightening the screening material. Hand-stretch the material and staple along the two remaining sides. Then re-attach the molding strips, using new finish nails, staples or brads.

4. If you have an aluminum doorframe, lay a new piece of spline in the groove on one of the narrow sides. Gently stretch the screen material and push the spline into place along the other narrow edge. (If the frame begins to bow, you can brace it by clamping a length of 1 x 4 along the long edges.) Finish up by rolling the spline into place on the remaining two sides, and trim the excess screen material with a utility knife or (for fiberglass screening) scissors.

> **TIP:**
> To protect that pristine new screening, invest in an inexpensive screen guard, available at glass-and-screen shops and most hardware stores. These expanded-metal protectors screw to the screen door's frame as a first line of defense against accidental bumps and tears. Our local glass shop pro prefers the over-size guard made for sliding patio door screens and uses them even on ordinary swinging-type screen doors.

Insert the upper right corner of the screen first.

Window Screens

Window screens are another common kid-tastrophe. With older, wooden-framed window screens, you may be able to re-screen the frames yourself using the same technique described above for screen doors. When it comes to the aluminum-framed screens typically found on sliding-type windows, how-ever, the frames are delicate and often not worth salvaging anyway. Shop around for the best price, and have a professional glass-and-screen shop make new ones.

One way to get an exact match is to take the old frame with you. If the frame is too badly mangled or is missing in action, however, you'll need to provide the shop with exact dimensions.

Here are the tools & materials you'll need to measure for screens:

measuring tape
ladder (if needed)
putty knife
pencil & paper

1. Working from the INSIDE, remove the sliding section of the window (unlatch, slide the window halfway open, and lift up until the bottom of the window clears the track). Stand the window up against a wall in a safe spot out of the way.

2. If the damaged screen is still in place, remove it. (You may need to use the putty knife to help pry the frame free. Since you're replacing it, you don't have to be particularly gentle with it, but be careful not to let an aluminum joint cut your fingers.)

3. To measure side-to-side, set the end of your tape measure against the flat side of the center mullion or into the groove provided for the screen. If there is a protruding screw or plastic tension bumper inside the groove, measure from the head of the screw or the face of the tension bumper.

> **TIP:**
> For tight little jobs like this, nothing beats a miniature tape measure. Look for a silver-dollar-sized pocket model with a narrow-width tape.

Then read the measurement where the tape grazes the *lip* of the track on the other side — the screen will need to clear that edge to slide into place. Deduct 1/8 inch from your measurement (1/4 inch if you measured to the face of a plastic tension bumper) to allow room to maneuver the screen into place.

4. Measure top-to-bottom in the same way, inserting the end of the tape measure up into the upper track, and reading the measurement at the lip of the bottom track. Again, deduct 1/8 inch.

5. Reinstall the sliding window by inserting the top edge into the top track and pushing upward until the bottom edge will clear the lower track.

6. Once you get your newly made aluminum-framed screens, you'll install them (just as you took them out) from the *inside* of the house. Remove the sliding window, and insert the *upper right* corner of the screen first. Push the frame tightly into the upper channel, then carefully work the rest of the screen into place. It's supposed to be a tight fit, so be prepared for a bit of a battle. Just be careful not to bend the aluminum frame.

Broken Windows

Your kid hit a home run — but the ball crashed right through your dining room window. After grounding her for a month and making dire (but probably soon-forgotten) threats to take it out of her allowance, what do you do?

If it's a huge picture window, or the fixed side of an aluminum-framed slider-type window, it's probably best to **call in an expert.** Large pieces of glass can get quite expensive, and I prefer to let someone else bear the risk of a crack while transporting that huge sheet of glass and setting it in place. Aluminum-framed windows will require disassembly and a special gasket, and (in colder climates) may contain special double- or even triple-pane glass. If it's the sliding section that's broken, however, you can at least save the cost of a house call by (carefully!) removing the window section and taking it to the glass shop yourself.

Broken glass in wood-framed or metal casement (crank-type) windows, however, is usually a pretty simple do-it-yourself repair.

Here are the tools & materials you'll need to get started:

gloves
protective goggles
ladder
screwdriver
duct tape
heat gun
cardboard box to dispose of glass shards
pliers
tape measure
glazing compound★
glazier's points (wood window frames)
glazing clips (metal frames)
putty knife
linseed oil or wood primer (wood frames)
rust-resistant paint (metal frames)
sandpaper or steel wool
caulking gun & exterior grade caulk
small angled sash brush
paint

1. The first step is to remove the old broken glass and glazing materials. Make sure you are wearing heavy leather gloves and protective eyewear before beginning, and work from the outside of the house. Carefully pick out any loose shards. If the window has not broken completely, it may be necessary to crack the glass a bit more. Tape liberally with duct tape to hold the glass together, then crack remaining sections with a hammer. Toss glass shards into a sturdy cardboard box or metal trash can for later disposal.

2. Once you've plucked out the "easy pickings," you may find some recalcitrant shards of glass still well-stuck around the edges. Softening the old glazing compound with a heat gun may make these pieces easier to remove. Use your putty knife to scrape away the old compound.

3. When all the old glass has been removed, use your putty knife to scrape away any remaining glazing compound, and pry out any triangular metal "glazier's points" that are still

> **★TIP:**
> All-purpose glazing compounds work fine for either wood or metal window frames. If you're glazing many panes in a metal frame, however, look for a putty made especially for metal windows — it is formulated to dry to a harder consistency.

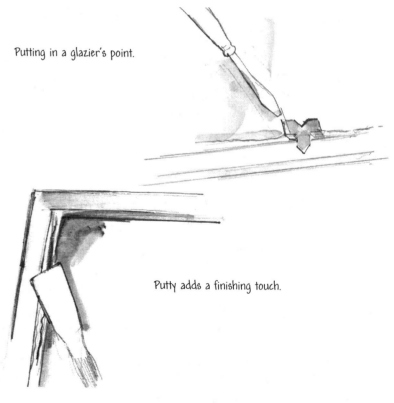

Putting in a glazier's point.

Putty adds a finishing touch.

Both putty and glazier's points help hold glass in place.

left in place using a small screwdriver or pliers. (On metal casement windows, you may encounter small wire tension clips instead.)

4. Measure the length and width of the frame's opening. Deduct 1/8 inch all the way around to provide room for expansion and contraction.

   Typically, residential window glass will be grade A or grade B sheet glass, measuring 3/32 inch to 1/8 inch in thickness. If you have any question about the type of glass you need, take a small piece of the old glass with you to the store. (Tape the edges with masking or duct tape for safety.)

5. Prepare the "rabbet" (the lip of the window that will accept the new glass) by sanding and sealing the surface. You can use a wood primer, linseed oil, or even a spritz of WD-40 for wooden frames; use rust-resistant paint on metal frames.

6. Apply a thin layer of glazing compound with your putty knife or (even easier) squirt a small bead of caulk around the edge where the glass will sit. Then fit the new pane in place, squeezing it gently into the glazing compound or caulk. Use your putty knife to press glazier's points (or, for metal windows, insert spring tension clips) around the edge to hold the glass in place.

7. To finish the glazing job, you'll need to add a nice, neat bevelled layer of putty around the edge of the glass. One way to apply the putty is to roll a golf-ball sized daub of glazing compound between your palms to make a thick

rope, then press the rope gently in place around the edge of the glass. Our local glass shop professional prefers to simply work a ball of putty in his hand until it is warm, then cups the ball in his palm, and scrapes his palm against the rabbet edge to apply the putty.

Once you have a rough layer of putty all around the window edge, smooth it with your putty knife. Hold the knife at a 45-degree angle, and press firmly. For the most professional look, draw the knife in one continuous motion from corner to corner before lifting the blade.

> **TIP:**
> To keep the glazing compound from sticking to your putty knife, coat the blade with mineral spirits. Even water can help in a pinch.

8. Allow the glazing compound to dry thoroughly. (Follow manufacturer's directions — usually about a week.) Then protect it by painting with a small, angled sash brush, using exterior paint that matches the window frames.

A Latch in Time

Child-proof latches, of course, are no substitute for diligent parental supervision. But there are a wide variety of ingenious devices on the market designed to keep curious toddlers away from that l-o-o-ong list of household "no-no's."

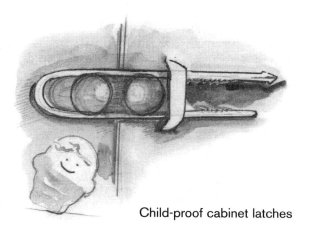

Child-proof cabinet latches

Drawer & Cabinet Latches

- For cabinet doors that have two knobs or handles side by side, a simple *U-shaped latch* requires no tools at all to install — simply pinch the flexible plastic arms and slide the connecting bar down until one end releases.

- A variation on that theme is a *tie-wrap-style latch*, with a toothed strap that's easy to tighten but requires a screwdriver to loosen (just press the release tab in a small slot). These latches require you to depress a button at the same time as you pull on the tab end to release the latch.

- Springy, one-piece *metal latches* screw to the inside of your cabinet door or drawer (make a pilot hole first with drill); they also require you to mount "catch" screws at an angle on the inside of the drawer or cabinet opening. A hole in the metal latch engages the screw to keep babies at bay; to release the latch, adults simply push down firmly on the spring metal.

- *Two-step plastic latches* require you to pinch the ribbed sides of the latch together and push down at the same time to release the latch. These devices mount to the inside of a cabinet door or drawer using small Phillips-head screws, and grip the cabinet's overhang (a screw-on catch is also provided in case your cabinet has a flat surface).

> **TIP:**
> Bringing the baby to visit friends or relatives? Thick rubber bands looped around a pair of cabinet door pulls are a quick, temporary deterrent.

Appliances & Toilets

Adjustable-length *plastic strap-and-buckle latches* can help keep toddlers from opening refrigerator doors and toilet lids. Simple to install, the straps and buckle attach with self-adhesive strips. Wherever possible, stick them to the appliance itself (they're not recommended for use on wallpaper, wallboard, or contact paper). To release the buckle, simply depress a pair of catches on either side. Consider attaching one to your medicine chest as well!

Kids' Workshops

Some local hardware stores now sponsor do-it-yourself seminars tailored expressly for kids. Stores in the Home Depot chain, for example, sponsor a "Kids' Workshop" one Saturday of each month to teach kids simple home do-it-yourself skills and safety pointers. Call the store nearest you for schedule and details, or visit http://www.homedepot.com.

Outlet Covers

There are several easy-to-install devices that can help keep prying fingers out of electrical outlets. *Plastic caps* simply plug in to cover vacant outlet openings. *Hinged* varieties are also available — just lift one side if you want to use an outlet, without fear you'll misplace a cap.

For a somewhat more permanent installation, try a *plug cover* — a molded plastic box that covers both the outlet and the plugs of appliances in use at that outlet. Just remove the center screw of the existing flat outlet cover, route the electrical cords through notches at the bottom of the new plug cover, and screw in place with the longer screw provided (a plastic tube helps support the box on the back side).

Corner Bumpers

Soft plastic bumpers adhere with double-sided tape to help protect toddlers from sharp furniture and cabinet edges. Make certain the surface you're applying them to is clean and free of wax or furniture polish to ensure good adhesion.

Chapter 5
COPING WITH HOUSEHOLD EMERGENCIES & HAZARDS

If your elementary school experience was like mine, you probably remember those seemingly endless fire drills. But for some reason we never seem to think about the possibility of emergencies at home. Would you know how to turn the water off if your plumbing suddenly started to look like Niagara Falls? Do your kids know what to do if they smell gas — and you're not home?

Because plumbing breaks, weather disasters and other emergencies can strike when we least expect them, it's important to practice NOW. Hold a "pre-need" drill to make sure that everyone in your home knows what to do when a household emergency arises. Then repeat the drill in six months — and six months after that.

You'll obviously want to talk about fire safety and plan escape routes. Here's a list of additional topics you may want to cover:

1. **How to Use a Fire Extinguisher:** You DO have a fire extinguisher in the house, don't you? If not, put it on your shopping list right now. Better yet, buy at least three so you can keep one handy in your kitchen, garage, and car.

   If your children are old enough to learn how to operate a fire extinguisher, teach them the basics and let them actually practice. Try outside in the back yard to help minimize the powdery mess, or call a local extinguisher re-charge service (look in the yellow pages under Fire Extinguishers) and ask if they hold fire safety classes for children. If you practice at home, don't forget to have your extinguisher recharged when you're through!

   Remember to stress that your child's own safety is paramount — fire extinguishers are only for small household fires. Tell your kids in no uncertain terms that you don't want or expect them to be heroes. If the fire is bigger than a breadbox, they should call for help.

Fire Extinguisher Ratings

A – wood and upholstery
B – flammable liquids (grease, paint, etc.)
C – electrical fires

For home use, select an "ABC" or "BC" type extinguisher. Models designed for home use will typically hold 2-1/2 to 7 pounds of dry chemical. If a gauge is provided on the extinguisher, check the pressure monthly. Recharge at least every 2 years and (of course) after any use.

Extinguishing Kitchen Fires

Is dinner fast on its way to becoming a charcoal briquet? You may be able to suffocate small stove-top fires by simply clapping on a lid, which will deprive the flames of oxygen.

If that doesn't work, your best bet for putting out a small cooking fire is an ABC or BC-class fire extinguisher. In a pinch, you can try baking SODA (but *not* baking POWDER), or even salt. Turn off the burner and the range hood fan if you can safely reach the controls.

Avoid the temptation to throw water on a cooking fire – you may wind up actually spreading the fire by sending flaming grease particles flying everywhere. Steam and grease spatters can also result in serious skin burns.

If you should encounter an ELECTRICAL fire in a stove, small appliance or house wiring, don't take chances – dial 911 immediately. For smouldering appliances or extremely small, self-contained fires, you may want to try shutting off the main breaker at your electrical panel and dousing the problem area with an ABC or BC-rated extinguisher while you're waiting for emergency assistance to arrive. If the fire is well-established, however, don't hang around and try to play fireman. Leave the house and use a neighbor's phone to call for help.

2. The Smell of Gas & Other Danger Signals: Make sure your kids recognize the odor of natural gas and equate that smell with danger. But be careful to explain that not all dangerous gasses can be detected with the nose. Carbon monoxide build-up (from operating a gasoline-powered engine in a confined space, for example) is odorless but can kill with little warning.

Walk around the house with your children and demonstrate what they might do if they detect such warning signals as smoke, a door that's warm to the touch, or feelings of light-headedness.

3. The Safest Spots in Case of Natural Disasters: If you live in an area that's subject to earthquakes, flooding, hurricanes or tornadoes, make sure your family knows the safest spots in and around your home to ride out Nature's furies. In earthquake-prone zones, for example, most experts recommend you seek shelter under a desk, table, or other heavy piece of furniture and stay AWAY from windows, large pictures or bookcases. If you live in an area where tornadoes or hurricanes are prevalent, a basement or storm shelter may be your safest option.

Emergency preparedness information is sometimes provided in the introductory pages to your local telephone book. Or check for an Office of Emergency Services in your city or county that can send you information on how to prepare for and survive a natural disaster.

4. How to Call for Help: Even very young children can be taught to dial 911 in medical and other emergencies. Make sure there's a phone within easy reach — and that they understand very clearly that the 911 service is for serious emergencies ONLY.

Take a few minutes to find out how to reach your local gas, electric, and water companies in case of utility-related problems. Your utility bill will usually include a 24-hour service number, or call customer service and ask how to contact their emergency repair division. Post those numbers by each telephone in the house, or tape them to the phone itself.

5. When Contact Is Broken: Not everyone may be at home when a natural disaster strikes. Agree ahead of time on an out-of-area friend or relative who can act as a coordinator if various members of the family become separated. (Since local telephone service may be disrupted within a disaster area, someone who is out-of-state or at least out of your immediate area may be easier to reach.) Write down the name and phone number of the designated contact person, and make sure everyone in the family has a copy to carry in their wallet or school backpack.

Call your children's school to find out what policies they have developed for emergency situations, and make sure your children are aware of what that might entail. The school's disaster plan might call for children to be assembled in a safe central location, such as the school cafeteria, for example. Reassure your children that you'll be there to pick them up as soon as humanly possible, and that other adults will be there to take care of them in the meantime.

CHECKLIST: Assembling an Emergency Kit

Emergency supplies can literally mean the difference between life and death. Here is a short checklist to help you assemble the basics:

- first-aid kit
- ABC-type fire extinguisher
- blankets or sleeping bags
- bottled water in unbreakable containers (at least 3-5 gallons per person—and don't forget to include extra for pets!)
- water purification tablets or chlorine bleach
- soap
- canned and/or dried food (check camping goods store for back-packers' supplies)
- mechanical can-opener
- cooking & eating utensils
- camp stove & fuel
- Swiss-army-type pocket knife
- crescent wrench
- water shut-off (T-handle type)
- candles and/or lanterns
- matches (protect in a waterproof container)
- flashlight & batteries
- portable radio & batteries
- heavy-duty plastic trash bags

Keep emergency supplies where you can reach them quickly, and mark a reminder on your calendar to check water, food and batteries every six months or so for freshness.

In addition to assembling an emergency supply kit for your home, stow a few basic items (such as a first-aid kit, flashlight, blanket, and bottled water) in your car.

Children's Safety Web Sites

The internet has a unique way of making safety topics interesting and fun. Here are some web sites designed with kids in mind:

Consumer Product Safety Commission:
http://www.cpsc.gov/cpscpub/pubs/chld-sfy.html
http://www.cpsc.gov/cpscpub/pubs/shower/shower.html
http://www.cpsc.gov/kids/kids.html
Download child safety brochures, tips for organizing a baby safety shower, and information for kids on safe bicycling, skating, and skateboarding.

Federal Emergency Management Area (FEMA) for Kids:
http://www.fema.gov/
Click on the "FEMA for Kids" tornado icon for emergency preparedness information tailored for kids.

Kids' Fire Safety Page:
http://www.firefighting.com/911/911kid/
This site links to Smokey The Bear's Official Home Page, coloring pages, quizzes, etc.

Both for emergencies and to accomplish some home repairs, you may need to know how to shut off the water, electricity, or gas to your home. While children generally shouldn't be entrusted with such chores, it's not a bad idea to let older children watch so they know where shut-offs are located and the basic procedure involved. Be sure to emphasize safety precautions (especially around the electrical panel), and encourage them to find another adult to help if an emergency should occur when you're not home.

How to Shut Off Water

As we mentioned in the plumbing chapter, there are at least one and sometimes two places where you typically can shut off the water to your entire house. You will most likely find a shut-off valve at or near your water meter. (For meters recessed into an inground box, you may need to lift the lid to find the valve.) There may also be a shut-off valve near where the water supply line enters your house — either inside (usually in the basement, if you have one), or outside near your foundation.

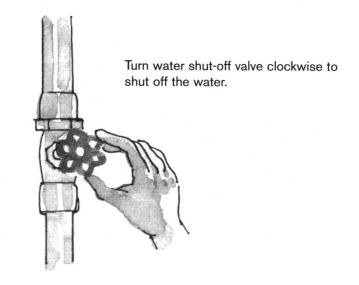

Turn water shut-off valve clockwise to shut off the water.

Typically, water shut-off valves found in or around your home look something like the round-handled faucet for a garden hose. Occasionally they may have a lever-like handle instead (a ball-valve). Both of these types of valves can be turned off by hand — simply turn clockwise (for round-handled valves) or crosswise to the pipe (for ball-valves) to shut the water off.

Valves at or near the water meter also may have a round handle, or they may simply look like a protruding tab on a circular base (somewhat akin to a miniature oven knob). This type of shut-off will require a crescent wrench or a pair of long-handled adjustable pliers to turn. (For deeply-recessed meters, you may need a long-handled "T"-type wrench to reach the tab.) Rotate the tab until it is perpendicular (crosswise) to the direction of the pipe to shut off the water.

On some occasions, you only need to turn off the water supply feeding a particular appliance such as the hot water heater or a faucet. A hot water heater will generally have one round-handled shut-off valve located above the heater, which controls the cold water coming in to be heated. There may also be a second shut-off valve that lets you close off the supply of hot water coming out of the heater and going to the house. When in doubt, shut them both off (turn handles clockwise).

You'll also find round handle-type shut-offs for water supply lines to faucets and toilets (which are called, logically enough, "water stops"). Just rotate clockwise to turn the water off.

How to Shut Off Electricity

We've already covered this in some detail in the chapter on electricity, and if you haven't already followed the directions to locate the main breaker and identify the various circuits in your home, I'd encourage you to do so now.

To summarize briefly: for houses with circuit breakers, simply flip the main breaker on your electrical panel to OFF. (If no main breaker is provided on your panel, you may need to flip each individual breaker to the OFF position instead.) Homes with a fuse-box system may have a main shut-off lever (often located on the outside of the box), or may require you to pull out a tray of fuses.

> ⚠ **CAUTIONS & CAVEATS:**
> Don't try to touch the electrical box if the floor or the box are wet (for example, in the middle of torrential rains or in a plumbing emergency). Call your utility company instead.

How to Shut Off Gas

If your home is served by NATURAL GAS, the shut-off valve will be located on the pipe close to your gas meter. Look

> ## ⚠ CAUTIONS & CAVEATS:
>
> LP gas is heavier than air, so if you smell a gas leak inside your home be sure to keep pets AND of course humans away from the basement.
>
> Gas leaks can present an explosion hazard. If you smell or hear escaping gas, get everyone outdoors as quickly as possible. Do not light a match or cigarette. Even flicking a light switch or using the phone may be hazardous. Ventilate your home well once the problem has been solved.

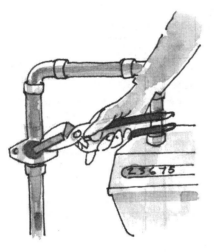

Turn protruding tab at meter crosswise (perpendicular) to pipe to shut off the flow of gas.

for a protruding tab on a circular base (like a small oven knob). When the gas is on, the tab will be in line with the pipe. To turn off the gas, use a crescent wrench or channel joint pliers to turn the tab crosswise (perpendicular) to pipe.

PROPANE (LP) gas tanks will generally have a shut-off knob or lever located on top of the tank. Turn clockwise to shut off.

Smoke Detectors

Smoke detectors are a valuable first line of defense against fire-related damage and injury. In some parts of the country, they're now required by law in both new residential construction and in any existing home that's being sold to a new owner.

So how many smoke detectors do you need? Experts recommend installing a separate smoke alarm in each bedroom, hall and stairwell, near the kitchen, and in the attic and basement.

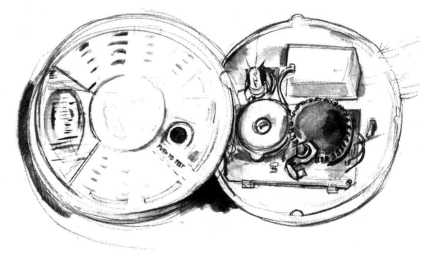

Change batteries in smoke detectors every six months or as directed from the manufacturer.

There are two basic types of smoke detectors: battery-operated and "hard-wired." Battery-powered models are the easiest to install — you can mount them virtually anywhere with just a screw or two. But you *will* have to change those batteries. Typically, the unit will "chirp" at you when batteries run low, but experts recommend changing batteries when you re-set your clocks for the beginning and end of Daylight Savings Time.

TIP:

If you find that one smoke alarm in your home is particularly prone to false alarms (from cooking vapors, for example), consider relocating the alarm to a different part of the room, or ask your hardware store clerk to recommend an alarm model that uses a different sensing mechanism.

Hard-wired smoke detectors must be connected into your home's wiring, a job that requires a certain amount of electrical expertise, some wire-fishing and, in many areas, a permit. Although hard-wiring avoids the nuisance of changing batteries, some models thoughtfully provide a battery back-up to ensure that the unit will continue to function during a power outage. Some hard-wired units also contain an extra wire allowing a series of smoke detectors to be interconnected, so that if one alarm is triggered they'll all go off (a feature that's required for new construction under some electrical codes).

Battery-operated smoke alarms generally work just fine as long as you don't pull the batteries to stop that annoying "chirp" — and then forget to replace them! If you do decide to use hard-wired alarms, I'd recommend you **call in an expert** to make sure the job is done correctly and to code.

Testing for Hazardous Substances

Toxic substances aren't just a problem for business and industry. From the solder in your plumbing to the gasses in your garage, what you don't see CAN hurt you.

A wide variety of home testing kits have recently hit the market, which allow consumers to check radon, carbon monoxide, lead, water quality and even EMF (electromagnetic field) levels in and around the home. Some of the literature that comes with these kits is downright scary. The manufacturers, after all, are making the very best case they can for you to use their products.

On the other hand, the dangers from lead, carbon monoxide and other toxic substances can be very real. For the most part, these do-it-yourself tests provide a fast, accurate, and relatively inexpensive way to help you evaluate the dangers in your home. And knowledge, as they say, is power.

Radon

Radon, an invisible, odorless gas, is a radioactive byproduct of naturally-decomposing uranium. Radon is the second leading cause of lung cancer in the US (trailing only cigarette smoking as a cause of lung cancer deaths) and is present in one in fifteen homes, according to one test kit manufacturer.

Home test kits allow you to test for the presence of radon as it seeps into your house from the ground or for radon gas that may be present in well water. Both types of test kit require you to mail in samples and pay a small additional laboratory test fee. Results are promised by mail within seven days.

Lead

Lead is one of the five most serious environmental threats to US children, according to a recent study by the Natural Resources Defense Council. More than 200,000 children in the US are affected by lead poisoning each year, and the Centers for Disease Control has estimated that nearly 900,000 US children between the ages of one and five have elevated levels of lead in their blood.

While chances of recovery are good if the problem is detected early, long-term exposure to lead can result in a lower IQ, reading and learning disabilities — even death. Adults, too, can suffer serious effects from lead poisoning, including muscular irregularities and abdominal pain.

Unfortunately, lead was a common coating for or ingredient in many building materials before its dangers became fully understood. Homes built before about 1930 frequently contained lead plumbing pipes. Lead was a common ingredient in oil-based house paint until it was banned for consumer use in 1978. And lead-based solder was used to join copper plumbing fittings as recently as 1986. Lead may also be present in improperly-glazed dishes, lead crystal glassware, lead-soldered food tins, and some vinyl miniblinds. Test-kit manufacturers estimate that five out of seven homes contain dangerous levels of lead.

Manufacturers offer a variety of products that allow you to check both solid objects and drinking water for the presence of lead. One stick-type indicator test kit, for example, reacts chemically to the presence of lead on surfaces such as dishes or glassware by turning the marker end a tell-tale pink or red color. Another manufacturer's kit allows you to mail paint chips or sanding dust for analysis by a professional lab. Tests that measure the lead content of tap water are also available (with either at-home or by-mail results, depending on the manufacturer).

Some household items that you might want to check for lead include:

• vinyl miniblinds, particularly in a child's room
• paint (especially if you're planning to do any sanding or renovation)
• your favorite coffee mug
• dishes and play tea sets (particularly old china, homemade ceramics, and any crazed, cracked or chipped pieces)
• lead crystal glassware, decanters or serving dishes
• bathtubs
• tap water

Carbon Monoxide

Carbon monoxide is a colorless, odorless gas produced as a byproduct of combustion. An insidious killer, carbon monoxide (or "CO" in chemists' language) binds to receptors in your blood that normally carry oxygen, causing headaches, dizziness, nausea and fatigue.

Common causes of carbon monoxide poisoning include malfunctioning or improperly vented space heaters, furnaces, fireplaces, and even gas clothes dryers or ranges.

There is a surprisingly wide variety of carbon monoxide detectors on the market, from battery-operated table-top models to hard-wired units (with or without battery back-up) that utilize your house current for power. Some newer dual-purpose designs combine both a smoke alarm and carbon monoxide detector within the same unit.

Like smoke alarms, the battery-operated carbon monoxide detectors are simple to install yourself — most mount with just a screw or two. Be sure to follow the manufacturer's instructions regarding placement of the unit. Some manufacturers recommend keeping the alarm at least fifteen feet from any source of combustion and avoiding areas like the garage, where the alarm may be exposed to high humidity or vapors from chemical solvents.

Because hard-wired models require you to tap into the existing house wiring, manufacturers typically recommend that you hire a qualified electrician to install them.

Water Quality

Not quite sure what's in your tap water? In addition to the kits that monitor for lead (see above), at least one manufacturer makes a water quality test kit that measures chlorine, pH and hardness levels, nitrate/nitrites, and iron content in your water.

Radiation & Electromagnetic Fields

Maybe it's from watching too many bad sci-fi movies, but I've always been just a LITTLE bit worried about the possibility of stray radiation from my microwave. If you share my nervous-nelly tendencies, there are now re-usable sensor cards that can monitor microwave leakage and put your mind at ease — or confirm that it's time to pitch the old "nuker."

You may also have been reading a lot about "electromagnetic fields" lately — a form of energy created by televisions, cellular telephones, computers and other plug-in electronic devices. Battery-operated EMF detectors can help you determine a safe distance from such radiation sources. Paranormal researchers reportedly are even using one such device to track EMF-emitting ghosts!

CONCLUSION

No one book can say it all, of course. I highly encourage you to check out other home repair manuals — your bookstore's shelves are loaded with them. Handy friends, relatives, and that ever-helpful guy or gal at your local hardware store are great sources of information and encouragement. And for specific problems or questions, try the manufacturer hotlines, web sites, and other links in the Resources section at the end of this book.

My greatest hope is that this book will help inspire women (and perhaps even a man or two) to tackle a home repair project that they used to believe was inaccessible, and to discover (as I did) that it's do-able — and even fun!

Now if you'll excuse me — there's a drippy faucet in our bathroom that's calling my name...

GLOSSARY

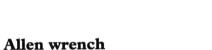

Allen wrench
Small, typically L-shaped plumbing tool with a hexagonal end.

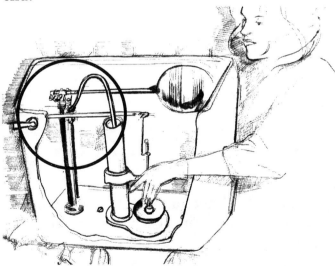

Ballcock assembly
Toilet mechanism that regulates flow of water into the tank.

Basin wrench
A long-handled wrench for removing the nuts underneath a sink that hold the faucet in place.

C-clamps
As the name implies, a "C"-shaped clamp that tightens (usually with a thumbscrew) to hold material in place while you work.

Channel joint pliers
See Pliers, adjustable.

Circuit
A wiring loop that powers a group of lights, appliances, or outlets within a house.

Cleat

A board that is nailed or tacked on the outside of a surface.

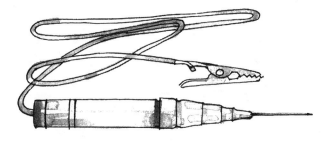

Continuity tester

An electrical device that generates a small flow of electricity, allowing you to ascertain whether two wires are connected to each other. (Also called an electrical tester.)

Crescent wrench

An adjustable plumbing tool for removing or tightening nuts, pipe connections, etc.

Cutting-End Nippers

A type of pliers with a rounded cutting face.

Diagonal cutters

A scissor-like tool for cutting wire or sheet metal. (Also called dikes.)

Drain cleaner

A rotating drum that turns a metal cable, used to feed down plumbing pipes to remove or push through the source of a clog.

Drywall knife

A flat-bladed tool used to apply and smoothe drywall mud, patching plaster, etc.

Electrical tester — see continuity tester

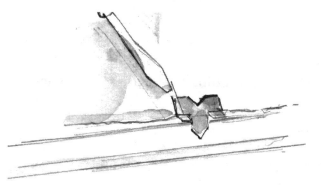

Glazier's points

Small, often triangular-shaped metal tabs used to hold glass in place in wooden-sash windows.

Ground

The leg of an electrical circuit that ultimately returns to the earth, by connecting to a buried metal stake or "ground rod." Ground wires are typically bare copper or color-coded green.

Hacksaw
A saw with a fine-toothed metal blade generally used for cutting through small metal objects such as plumbing pipe, screws, bolts, etc.

Hard-wired
Connected directly and permanently to household wiring as a source of power, rather than from a battery or plug.

Hot
The leg of an electrical circuit that provides power and, consequently, that has the potential to shock you. Hot wires are conventionally color-coded black.

Joint compound
Also known as "drywall mud," joint compound is applied wet to cover and finish taped joints between sheets of drywall and may also be troweled on to provide texture. A finer, easier-to-sand variety known as "topping compound" may be used as a finish coat.

Joist
A wooden framing member used to support floors or ceilings.

Low-Voltage
An electrical system often used for outside lighting, doorbells, etc. in which the standard 110-volt household current is "stepped down" to a significantly lower voltage by use of a transformer.

Mildecide
A chemical additive for paint that retards the growth of mildew.

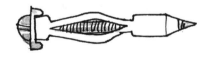

Molly bolt
A fastener for use with drywall and hollow-core doors.

Monkey wrench
A plumbing tool similar to a pipe wrench except without serrations on the jaws.

Nailset
A carpenter's tool that resembles a small punch, used for "setting" (recessing) the nailhead below the surrounding surface.

Needlenose pliers
As the name implies, a type of pliers with long, skinny jaws.

Neutral
The "return" leg of an electrical circuit that carries current back to the panel and, ultimately, a grounding bar. Neutral wires are typically color-coded white.

Packing
One of several methods for keeping water from traveling up a faucet's valve stem and seeping out around the faucet handle. Some faucets use an O-ring or a packing washer for this purpose; in others, packing material is wound around the stem.

Paint screen
A wire mesh panel made to hook over the edge of a paint bucket as a convenient way for the painter to remove excess paint from a roller.

Patching plaster
Usually a dry powder made to be mixed with water and then used to repair holes or cracks in plaster.

Phillips screwdriver
A type of screwdriver characterized by the cross-shaped pattern on its tip.

Pipe wrench
A heavy plumbing wrench with adjustable, serrated jaws.

Pliers, adjustable
Also known as "channel joint," this type of pliers has a slotted adjustment in one handle that allows the user to adjust the jaws' gripping distance.

Pliers, blunt-nosed
An electrical tool used for gripping, twisting, and cutting wire.

Plumber's putty
A resilient, non-hardening, putty-like substance used to prevent leakage around drains, drain line connections, and other non-pressurized metal-to-porcelain or metal-to-metal applications.

Putty knife
A small, flat-bladed tool used to apply putty or patch small holes.

Rabbet
The indented lip around the inside edge of a wooden window frame, designed to hold window glass.

Razor knife
A cutting tool that uses a razor blade as its cutting edge. For safety's sake, look for one with a retractable blade.

Ringer equivalence number (REN)
A telephone industry standard that indicates the amount of power needed to activate the ringer on that particular model of telephone. (Most telephone companies supply enough power through a standard residential phone line to ring multiple phones provided their REN numbers total 5 or less.)

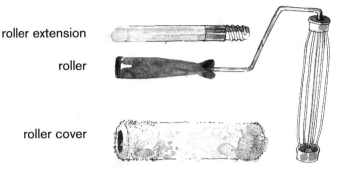

roller extension

roller

roller cover

Roller extension
A screw-on extension handle for a paint roller.

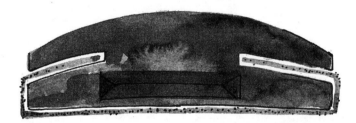

Sanding block
A hand-held finish tool designed to hold a sheet (or partial sheet) of sanding paper.

Seat
A cupped brass fitting inside a faucet against which a washer is tightened to seal off the flow of water.

Spackle
A wall-patching material used for filling holes and smoothing over minor imperfections.

Spline
A round, cord-like material that is wedged into a groove to hold screening material in place.

Studfinder
A battery-operated sensing device used to locate studs and other framing members inside walls.

Teflon tape
A thin, ribbon-like plumbing material used to help ensure leak-free connections on water and (sometimes) gas fittings.

Terminal screw
A mounting screw designed to tighten down and hold an electrical wire in place.

Trap
A bent pipe arrangement typically found under sinks and tubs, for example, intended to "trap" water to prevent the escape of sewer gasses.

Vent
A pipe leading up and away from drain lines to allow sewer gasses to escape.

Visegrips
A type of locking pliers.

Waterstop
The valve that turns water on and off to a fixture such as a toilet or sink faucet.

Wire nuts
A round cap, often with a grooved or coiled metal interior, made to screw over and protect a wire connection.

Wire strippers
A scissor-like electrical tool used to remove the insulating plastic coating from electrical wires.

RESOURCES

The following sources should give you a good starting place for many product, installation and safety questions. While we've tried to include a wide variety of useful sources, it's obviously impossible to list each and every quality manufacturer or helpful hotline. To anyone who may be left out, our apologies.

Please note: Inclusion on this list is NOT intended as a product endorsement or recommendation of any kind.

MANUFACTURER HOTLINES

ADHESIVES:
- Armstrong/Henry
  (800) 232-4832
  P.O. Box 3233
  Lancaster, PA 17604-3233
  http://www.stickwithus.com or
  http://www.armstrong.com

CAULK:
- DAP, Inc.
  (800) 543-3840
  855 N. Third Street
  Tipp City, OH 45371
  http://www.DAP.com

CEILING FANS:
- Aloha Housewares
  (maker of Hampton Bay, Galleria, and others)
  (800) 295-4448
  P.O. Box 420386
  Dallas, TX 75342-0386
  e-mail: ahi@aol.com

CHILD-PROOFING:
  The First Years, Inc.
  (800) 533-6708
  One Kiddie Drive
  Avon, MA 02322-1171

CLEANING, STAIN & ODOR REMOVAL PRODUCTS:

- Beaumont Products Inc.
  (pet odor eliminators, all-purpose cleaners)
  (800) 451-7096
  1560 Big Shanty Road
  Kennesaw, GA 30144
  http://www.citrusmagic.com

- Magic American
  (maker of "Goo Gone" and cleaning products)
  (800) 321-6330
  23700 Mercantile Road
  Cleveland, OH 44122
  http://www.fairfield.com/magic/homepage.html

- National Sanitary Supply Co.
  (800) 428-9677 (I BUY NSS)
  13217 S. Figueroa
  Los Angeles, CA 90061
  http://www.nssc.com

CLOSET ORGANIZERS

- Clairson International
  (maker of "Closet Maid")
  (800) 874-0008
  650 SW 27th Avenue
  Ocala, FL 34474

- Lee Rowan
  (800) 325-6150 x0
  900 S. Highway Drive
  Fenton, MO 63026
  http://www.leerowan.com

ELECTRICAL:

- Leviton
  (800) 323-8920 customer service
  (800) 824-3005 tech support
  59-25 Little Neck Pkwy.
  Little Neck, NY 11362
  http://www.leviton.com

PAINTING:

- The Flood Company
  (maker of Emulsa-Bond® paint additive)
  (800) 321-3444
  P.O. Box 2535
  Hudson, OH 44236-0035
  http://www.floodco.com

- Masterchem Industries, Inc.
  (maker of KILZ® primer-sealer/stainblockers)
  (800) 325-3552
  P.O. Box 368
  Barnhart, MO 63012
  http://www.masterchem.com

PLUMBING FIXTURES:

- American Standard
  (800) 223-0068
  Attn: U.S. Plumbing Products
  1 Centennial Avenue
  P.O. Box 6820
  Piscataway, NJ 08855-6820
  http://www.americanstandard.com
  http://www.us.amstd.com/

- Eljer Industries
  (800) 423-5537
  14801 Quorum Drive
  Addison, TX 75240

- Kohler Co.
  (800) 456-4537
  (800-4-KOHLER)
  444 Highland Drive
  Kohler, WI 53044
  http://www.kohlerco.com

SAFETY PRODUCTS & TEST KITS:

- First Alert, Inc.
  (800) 392-1395 smoke alarms
  (800) 323-9005 CO detectors
  3901 Liberty Street Road
  Aurora, IL 60504
  http://www.firstalert.com

- Enzone USA
  (radon, lead and other test kits)
  (800) 448-0535
  P.O. Box 290480
  Davie, FL 33329-0480
  http://www.enzoneusa.com
  Consumers may also contact an affiliated organization, The Home Safety Institute [(800) ARE-U-SAFE], for questions and informative brochures.

- HybriVet Systems, Inc.
  (lead and oil/latex paint test kits)
  (800) 262-LEAD
  P.O. Box 1210
  Framingham, MA 01701

- Kidde Safety
  (fire extinguishers, smoke & CO detectors)
  (800) 654-9677
  1394 S. Third Street
  Mebane, NC 27302
  http://www.kidde.com

SPRINKLERS:

- Lawn Genie
  (800) 231-5117
  27631 La Paz Road
  Laguna Niguel, CA 92677
  http://www.lawngenie.com

- Rain Bird
  (800) 724-6247 (RAIN BIRD) tech support
  (800) 426-7782 design service
  7590 Britannia Court
  San Diego, CA 92173-3407
  http://www.rainbird.com

TOOLS:

- Craftsman
  (800) 682-8691
  Attn: Craftsman Club Mgr.
  3333 Beverly Road
  Hoffman Estates, IL 60179
  http://www.sears.com/craftsman

- Ryobi
  (800) 323-4615
  Attn: Customer Service
  1424 Pearman Dairy Road
  Anderson, SC 29625
  http://www.ryobi.com

- Stanley Tools
  (800) 262-2161
  600 Myrtle Street
  New Britain, CT 06053
  http://www.stanleyworks.com

HARDWARE CHAINS

- Home Depot
  http://www.homedepot.com

- Lowes
  http://www.lowes.com

- Orchard Supply Hardware
  http://www.osh.com

- TrueValue
  http://www.truevalue.com/index.asp

MAGAZINES

- The Family Handyman
  (612) 854-3000 editorial
  (800) 285-4961 subscriptions
  7900 International Drive, 9th Floor
  Minneapolis, MN 55425
  http://www.readersdigest.com

- Today's Homeowner
  (212) 779-5000 editorial
  (800) 456-6369 subscriptions
  2 Park Avenue, 9th Floor
  New York, NY 10016
  http://www.todayshomeowner.com

OTHER ON-LINE HELP

- http://www.tripod.com/living/staplegun
  A service provided by the San Diego Union-Tribune's web site which includes "Ask the Handy Girls" and various tool and fix-it tips.

- www.plumbnet.com/welcome.html
  The Interactive Plumbing Network — information on new products, code compliance, manufacturers, and more.

- www.housenet.com
  Gene & Katie Hamilton's web site provides advice on home improvement projects, lawn & garden, calculators, and much more.

- www.doityourself.com
  How-to information, Q&A forum, links.

- www.homecentral.com
  Plumbing and other repair information, calculators, links.

- www.hometime.com
  Affiliated with the popular TV show, this site contains a wide variety of home improvement and repair information.

- www.homeideas.com
  Brochures, articles, links (a joint project of Today's Homeowner magazine and "Build.com," a provider of on-line services to the building products industry).

- www.energyoutlet.com
  Energy conservation ideas.

- www.theplumber.com
  Plumbing advice, manufacturer links, FAQs, plumbing history and more in a searchable site.

- www.plumbingnet.com
  Huge collection of plumbing manufacturers; searchable message board.

- www.wp.com/paint
  Information on paint failures, surface prep, caulk and more.

- www.bhglive.com/homeimp
  As you'd expect from Better Homes & Gardens, a wonderfully extensive Encyclopedia of Home Improvement complete with illustrated directions for a variety of projects, a tool dictionary, project calculators, etc.

- www.rooter.com/plumber
  Free answers from a RotoRooter plumber.

- www.btplumber.com/onlinehelp.htm
  Helpful plumbing advice from Maine plumber Robert W. McClellan.

GOVERNMENT & NON-PROFIT ORGANIZATIONS

- Centers for Disease Control & Prevention
  Lead Poisoning Prevention Branch
  (888) 232-6789 for free publications on childhood lead poisoning.
  mailing address:
  Nat'l Center for Environmental Health
  Mailstop F42
  4770 Buford Highway
  Atlanta, GA 30341
  http://www.cdc.gov/nceh/programs/lead/lead.htm

- Consumer Product Safety Commission
  (800) 638-2772 for publications including free child-safety brochures, product recall information, and news releases.
  Washington, DC 20207
  http://www.cpsc.gov

- Federal Emergency Management Agency (FEMA)
  (800) 480-2520 for publications
  FEMA Distribution Center
  P.O. Box 2012
  Jessup, MD 20794-2012
  http://www.fema.gov

- National Safety Council's Lead Information Center
  (800) LEAD-FYI for informational packet
  (800) 424-LEAD for detailed information or questions
  1025 Connecticut Avenue NW #1200
  Washington, DC 20036-5405
  http://www.nsc.org/ehc/lead.htm

- National Safety Council's National Radon Information
  Hotline
  (800) SOS-RADON (767-7236)
  P.O. Box 33435
  Washington, DC 20033
  http://www.nsc.org/ehc/indoor/radon.htm

- US Environmental Protection Agency (EPA)
  401 M Street SW
  Washington, DC 20460
  http://www.epa.gov/opptintr/lead/index.html (lead programs)
  http://www.epa.gov/iaq/radon/rnxlines.html (radon)

INDEX